2

Dear Jan,

May God's Presence and
His "whispers of love"
be with you each day as
you continue to rejoice,
give thanks and sing.

Dorothy D. France
July 9, 2003

Blessed Assurance

Fifty-two Meditations
Inspired by
Familiar Hymns of the Church

Dorothy D. France

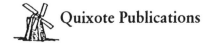 Quixote Publications

Library of Congress Cataloging-in-Publication Data

France, Dorothy D.
    Blessed assurance : fifty-two meditations based on favorite hymns
of the church / by Dorothy D. France.
        p.   cm.
    ISBN 0-9633083-8-6 (alk. paper)
    1. Hymns--Devotional use. 2. Christian Church (Disciples of
Christ)--Hymns--History and criticism.   3. Hymns, English--United
States--History and criticism.   I. Title.
BV340.F73   1998
264' .23--dc21   98-30803
                                                                CIP

Cover photo: Caribbean sunrise
                 Courtesy John and Deborah MacDonald
Author photo: Arnold's Photographers

To my two grandsons

David and Jason

who continue to fill

my life with joy and keep me singing

even during the darkest days

Also by Dorothy D. France

Newness of Life
Special Days of the Church Year
Partners in Prayer

Editor of *At Christ's Table*

O God, I know you don't go by the things I say but by the music played on the strings of my heart. Help me keep my heart in tune.

Amen.

Contents

Contents

Contents

Contents

Prelude

Through the years hymnals have contained a panorama of devotional literature gleaned from the lives and experiences of many writers. The words are the starting point! They remind us of God's care and love, bringing comfort, courage, assurance, and hope, along with words of salvation and new life. They reflect our faith and the faith of the Church, ever reminding us of our need and responsibility to speak often with the Lord and to tell his story to the nations.

In times of joy or uncertainty and in our moments of personal and corporate worship, words from our favorite hymns often inspire and cheer us when all else seems to have failed. They enable us to come to the garden and draw strength and hope from his presence.

May these meditations provide guidance in times of personal worship and be a helpful resource for leading others in worship. Many have been used successfully in times of worship before choir rehearsals. They can prove helpful for church school classes, women's and men's fellowships and family night hymn sings. Persons confined to their homes or nursing or retirement communities will welcome *Blessed Assurance* as a link with others with whom they once joined in worship. The book can also be presented as a gift to honor choir or worship leaders.

To all those musicians, choirs, and congregations who helped make the hymnal come alive for me over the years, I offer my appreciation. To Geneva Bohannon, I express my personal thanks for the many hours spent typing the original manuscript. I am grateful to Carl, my beloved husband, for his encouragement and assistance that made it possible for me to write.

Every effort has been made to identify and give credit to the authors whose material was included. To them and to the authors designated as unknown, I express my heartfelt thanks.

D. D. F

Bright Hope for Tomorrow

Rejoice in your hope, be patient in tribulation, be constant in prayer.
Romans 12:12

Pardon for sin and a peace that endureth,
thy own dear presence to cheer and to guide;
strength for today
and bright hope for tomorrow,
blessings all mine, with ten thousand beside!

Great Is Thy Faithfulness
Thomas O. Chisholm

When Robert Louis Stevenson was a small child, often he would press his face against the windowpane to watch the lamplighter come down the street. One evening he was asked what he was doing at the window, and his reply was, "I'm watching the lamplighter. He's punching holes in the darkness."

Hope enables us to punch holes in the darkness. It is one of our most valuable gifts. It blesses everything within our reach, and it sustains us with unfailing strength in the darkest hours of the night. One person described hope as "the gift that makes me hang on when I can't remember why I want to, when I can't find the flowers because of the mud."

Another person described hope as contagious and life-giving with the potential for transforming a crowd as when a favorite football team takes the lead in the final seconds of a game. It can also transform a family when the doctor advises that a kidney donor has been found for their child who is very ill.

Hope is a word we use many times each day, silently and orally, positively and negatively. However, distinguishing between hope and fantasy is important—between what J. B. Phillips, the author of *Good News*, calls hope and wishful thinking. "Hope," he writes," is based on realities—and in the end on God, the great reality. But wishful thinking, though it often sounds like hope, is nothing more than what we should like to happen." Realistic hope is the ability to desire and to expect that which is positive and possible in life.

Gerald Kennedy once told the story of an eight-year-old named Jeffrey who ended his grace for breakfast with the words, "We thank you for this beautiful day." His mother looked out the window at the approaching storm and asked him, "Why did you say that? This day is anything but beautiful." "Mother," he replied, "We should never judge a day by its weather."

Jeffrey, perhaps wise beyond his years, was expressing realistic hope for an enjoyable day regardless of the weather. Let us face tomorrow with hope in our hearts. The great days are not all past.

Prayer: O God, grant us patience to endure and faith to accept whatever comes with each new day. May we refuse to let hope die as we look forward to a better tomorrow. Amen.

Drive Our Fear and Doubt Away

O man of little faith, why did you doubt?
Matthew 14:31

*But let him ask in faith, with no doubting, for he
who doubts is like a wave of the sea that is driven
and tossed by the wind.*
James 1:6

Joyful, joyful, we adore thee,
God of glory, Lord of love;
hearts unfold like flowers before thee,
opening to the sun above.
Melt the clouds of sin and sadness,
drive our fear and doubt away;
giver of immortal gladness,
fill us with the light of day.

Joyful, Joyful We Adore Thee
Henry van Dyke

Bishop William Quayle told of lying awake, trying to
hold the world together by his worrying, when God
said, "Now William, you go to sleep and I'll sit up."

Doesn't this sound like us? We lie awake filled with doubts and fears, tossing, turning, and fretting about what we didn't do, should have done, can't get done, or what someone else could do better. We lie awake, anxious about the outcome of a job interview or a physical examination or how we will manage when our children are college age or we face retirement.

When we have doubts, or when we become obsessed with fears that make us want to turn and run away, perhaps what we need is a strong dose of an antidote called faith. We know it as a gift from God.

Much has been written about faith. C. H. Spurgeon penned some words of wisdom for us in a little book entitled *Gleanings Among the Sheaves*. He writes, "The way in which most people get their faith increase is by great trouble. We do not grow strong in faith on sunshiny days. It is in stormy weather that faith grows stronger . . . Look at the old oaks; how is it that they have become so deeply rooted in the earth? Ask the March winds, and they will tell you. It was not the April shower that did it, or the sweet May sunshine, but the rough wind shaking the tree to and fro, causing its roots to strike deeper and to take a firmer hold."

It takes the darkness of night to make the stars shine. Our faith, like the stars' brilliance, deepens within us as we live by it during the tough situations we confront.

> *God hath not promised skies always blue,*
> *Flower-strewn pathways all our lives through,*
> *God hath not promised sun without rain,*
> *Joy without sorrow, peace without pain.*

God hath not promised we shall not know
Toil and temptation, trouble and woe.
He hath not told us we shall not bear
Many a burden, many a care.
But God hath promised strength for the day,
Rest for the laborer, light for the way,
Grace for the trials, help from above
Unfailing sympathy, undying love.
Author Unknown

Prayer: O Lord, dispeller of darkness, teach us to make friends with our trials, and forgive us when we try to evade the difficult decisions that are placed before us. Each time we falter, may we be drawn closer to you as we replace the doubts that consume our hearts with faith and courage. Help us to learn that even in dark times, we can find reason to sing, "Joyful, Joyful, We Adore Thee." Amen.

Join Hands Then

Bear one another's burdens, and so fulfill the law of Christ.

Galatians 6:2

Join hands, disciples of the faith,
whate'er your race may be;
all children of the living God
are surely kin to me.

In Christ There Is No East or West
John Oxenham

A troop of Boy Scouts came across an abandoned section of railroad track during a hike in the woods. Each one tried walking the rails, but eventually each lost his balance and tumbled off.

Suddenly, two of the boys, after considerable discussion, offered to bet that they could both walk the entire track without falling off. The other members of the troop challenged them to make good on their boast. The two boys then jumped up on opposite rails, extended a hand to balance each other, and walked the entire section with no trouble whatsoever.

God created us so that we need one another. He knew that we could do things better, produce more, and live happier lives by helping one another.

Some years ago several Church World Service/CROP staff members were making an on-site visit to self-help projects organized in conjunction with the Church in the Dominican Republic. One evening the group was chatting and singing as the caravan of three jeeps proceeded slowly along a little traveled and poorly maintained road en route from Santa Domingo to a village several hours away. None of us realized how dark the night or how bright the vehicle lights until suddenly the headlights on the second jeep failed. Our Dominican guide, who was driving the lead vehicle, insisted that this would not be a problem. He stated with great confidence: "I'll drive on the right side of the road, the vehicle without lights will drive in the middle of the road, and the third jeep will drive to the left side of the road. This way the lights from the two will provide ample light for the third." The journey was completed without further interruption.

Someone has written that a snowflake isn't much by itself, but it takes a bulldozer to move them when they cooperate. How often we forget how weak we are alone and how powerful we can become when we join hands.

Prayer: Sometimes it is difficult for us, O Lord, to acknowledge our need for others. At times, our pride and even our prejudices hold us back until we are faced with a crisis. Touch our hearts with your love that we may reach out our hands to others in the good times and the bad. Amen.

Publish Glad Tidings

How beautiful upon the mountains
are the feet of him who brings
good tidings . . .
Isaiah 52:7

O Zion, haste, thy mission high fulfilling,
To tell to all the world that God is light,
That he who made all nations is not willing
One soul should perish,
lost in shades of night.
Publish glad tidings, Tidings of peace,
Tidings of Jesus, Redemption and release.

O Zion, Haste, Thy Mission High Fulfilling
Mary A. Thomson

An African proverb states that the only crime on the desert considered worse than murder is knowing where there is water and not telling. What is it about individuals that makes us keep good news to ourselves? Is it a habit that we have picked up from our surroundings, or does it stem from our own sense of insecurity that surfaces when others receive more honors or commendations than we do?

A colleague and longtime friend, the Reverend Donald Morrison, shared in his Christmas letter a discussion that took place in his study-prayer-action class. The members were discussing the tendency to look for the bad rather than the good in people and situations. Those in attendance agreed that the media was full of bad news and that media people, or so it seemed, were always looking for sensational news in which people are in hostile opposition with one another.

Someone in the class pointed out that even we as individuals often seem to relish taking someone apart with negative and sometimes hostile comments. At that point he wrote, "One of our class members commented jokingly that it would take all the fun out of it [life] if we couldn't or didn't do that. So it is," he continued, "that many of us relish hearing and focusing on the negative rather than the positive things about people and situations." He concluded, "It occurs to me, that there is need for an intentional pursuit of looking for the good."

Recently, when I answered the telephone, a neighbor, who is convinced that her calling in life is to be the bearer of bad news said, "Guess what? I'm improving. Today I'm calling to share some good news!" Here is an intentional pursuit of publishing glad tidings.

A witness is a powerful communicator. We witness as we spread the good news through our daily contacts and actions. Even though we are prone to communicate the bad, we ourselves like to be the recipients of the good. We read good news over and over again. The telegram or letter of congratulations is read until it is dog-eared. The note of love and friendship is read until the ink fades. The cards received when we are ill or hospitalized or a shut-in are posted on the refrigerator, mirror, or bulletin board as a constant source of encouragement and love. Ah, good news. What a blessing it is.

> *When life seems just a dreary grind,*
> *And things seem fated to annoy,*
> *Say, something nice to someone else*
> *And watch the world light up with joy.*
> Author Unknown

Prayer: Stir us, O Lord, that we might seek to have a part in the publishing of glad tidings. Amen.

With Every Step I Take

A man's mind plans his way,
but the LORD *directs his steps.*
Proverbs 16:9

Let peace begin with me;
let this be the moment now.
With every step I take,
let this be my solemn vow:
to take each moment and live each moment
in peace eternally.
Let there be peace on earth,
and let it begin with me.

Let There Be Peace on Earth
Sy Miller and Jill Jackson

A traveler in ancient Greece once lost his way and, seeking to find it, asked directions from a man who turned out to be Socrates. "How can I reach Mount Olympus?" asked the traveler. To this, Socrates replied: "Just make every step you take go in that direction."

We all remember times in our lives when we were uncertain of our direction and were afraid we would lose our way. The first step was the hardest, whether it was when we started to school, spent our first night away from home, started a new job, got married, began physical therapy, moved to a new neighborhood, or began a new life in retirement. No doubt we paused before each event to ask God to guide us and give us the strength we needed to begin.

The mistake we often make is to expect to see that guidance with all the answers for the future laid out before us. God usually does not make his will known very far in advance. Instead, his way is to guide us one step at a time. Perhaps he knows we would wander away from him if we did not have to depend on his love and wisdom each hour and each day.

An elderly man was taking his daily walk when he came upon a young boy who was holding for dear life to one end of a ball of string. The other end of the string was stretching upward toward the sky. "My child," he asked, "why are you still holding on to that string? The kite is out of sight." The boy replied, "I know it is there. I can still feel the tug of it."

There will be times when no visible signs of his presence will be evident in our lives. We will know only that he is there guiding us because we can still feel the tug on the string. As long as we have faith in his presence, we will be able to continue on life's journey, taking one step at a time until our goal is reached.

Prayer: Teach us a faith, O God, that will dispel our doubts. Enable us to face life with courage. Grant us wisdom and complete trust to follow your leading and to know that you will be beside us every step of the way. Amen.

Teach Me Thy Patience

But if we hope for what we do not see, we wait
for it with patience.

Romans 8:25

Teach me thy patience; still with thee
In closer, dearer company,
in work that keeps faith sweet and strong,
in trust that triumphs over wrong.

O Master, Let Me Walk with Thee
Washington Gladden

omeone has said that patience is being able to idle
your motor when you feel like stripping your
gears. That's me! The Lord says wait, but I want to
go and do right now.

Yet I know that Epictetus was right when he said, "No
great thing is created suddenly any more than a bunch of
grapes or a fig. If you tell me that you desire a fig," he continued, "I answer you that there must be time. Let it first
blossom, then bear fruit, then ripen."

We are all in such a hurry. Yet the best things that God has for us often take time and patience to mature. Patience is one of the most difficult attitudes to maintain, especially when things seem slow in working out. We want so much to prove our faith and to prove God's power that we sometimes become frustrated and impatient with ourselves and our efforts.

But patience means awaiting God's time without doubting his love. It is linked with faith and hope.

When answers to our prayers do not come instantly or results of our activities are not seen immediately, let us not conclude that they are not being answered or fulfilled. The patience required to wait may be painful because it requires restraint, silence, and inactivity. Sometimes we have to let the manifestations of our God come forth step by step. God is at work in ways we may not presently see, yet we are being guided and blessed.

Happy is the family
That knows how to live without haste,
With time for play and conversation,
And meditation that enriches the mind.

For the richest treasures
Are not found by hurry,
Nor can they be bought
By those who rush here and there;

But are found by patient search
Of those who dig deeply

And discover life's hidden riches,
And do not fail to notice
Those that are near at hand.
Author Unknown

Prayer: O God, you have been so patient with us. Forgive our impatience with ourselves. Forgive us for our continuous going about trying to hurry things along rather than seeking your guidance and waiting for your answers. Forgive our impatience with others and with you. Teach us how to bear the pain of patience. Amen.

Open My Eyes, Illumine Me

. . . having the eyes of your hearts enlightened, that you may know what is the hope to which he has called you . . .

Ephesians 1:18

Open my eyes, that I may see
glimpses of truth thou hast for me;
place in my hands the wonderful key
that shall unclasp and set me free.
Silently now I wait for thee,
ready, my God, thy will to see.
Open my eyes, illumine me,
Spirit divine!

Open My Eyes, That I May See
Clara H. Scott

S ome members of the Church Women United in Richmond, Virginia, were guests of the Salvation Army. Following a period of fellowship and overall orientation provided at the church, we traveled by Salvation Army vans to visit the Boys and Girls Club, the Alcohol and Drug Rehabilitation Center, and the halfway house for abused women. The trip took us through the Samarias of Richmond—the slum area housing projects, the boarded-up shops and houses, and the throngs of children playing in the streets while their mothers chatted with one another over decaying fences that separated one house from another.

As we rode along the narrow and less tended streets from one project to another, I overheard a woman sitting behind me remark to the person next to her, "Why couldn't they have taken us over the interstate route instead of through this horrible area? This depresses me. What do they expect us to do about it anyway?" Her companion replied, "Maybe there are others like me who need to be reminded every once in a while of how the other half lives. I guess there is always a little more we can do."

Many of us may feel like the woman who preferred to travel the interstate highway. After all, we have been bombarded with instant pictures of devastation caused by natural disasters such as floods, hurricanes, and earthquakes. Add to this the live portrayal of persons dying from starvation brought on by drought and greed. Then add the continuing ethnic conflicts that are tearing families and cities apart and the murders and assaults that are taking place right in our neighborhoods. We may not live close enough to the realities of these events to pull the shade down or close the blinds, but we resort to flipping the television channels or turning off the radio or even limiting our reading to the entertainment sections.

Some have indicated that we suffer from "compassion fatigue," that our love has simply become exhausted. This has caused us, perhaps without realizing it, to erect imaginary walls so that we will not know the burdens of others. We might sympathize with them in their misfortunes and may occasionally share our resources, but we do not really want to become involved.

We need compassion both for those far away and those next door. Showing love to those near at home may be the hardest because it calls us into personal involvement. Perhaps that is why the temptation to pull the shade down or close the blinds is so strong. When we are tempted to settle for something less than our best, to close our eyes to the needs of others, let us remember that Christ's was a love that never tired. He kept on loving and giving, even when his friends disappointed him and deserted him in his hour of need. Would that our love would never tire, and that we could see the world through God's eyes.

Prayer: Teach our eyes, O Lord, how to see the world as you see it. Touch us again and again until our vision is restored, and we see all human beings as your creation. Amen.

Make and Keep Me Pure Within

Blessed are the pure in heart, for they shall see God.
Matthew 5:8

Plenteous grace with thee is found,
grace to cover all my sin;
let the healing streams abound,
make and keep me pure within.
Thou of life the fountain art,
freely let me take of thee;
spring thou up within my
heart,
rise to all eternity.

Jesus, Lover of My Soul
Charles Wesley

A retired teacher now spends many of her days teaching English to newly arrived refugees from around the world. Watching her as she interacts so lovingly with her students is always inspiring. One day, just as she completed the morning class for Cambodian women, one of them approached her and said in broken English, "Miss Irene, I want what you have." Miss Irene, as she is affectionately called, wasn't sure what it was Maly wanted. She asked her if she wanted her sweater or blouse or scarf. Maly indicated that she wanted none of those. Miss Irene then asked Maly if she'd like her coat or maybe one like it. "No," was again the response. Then Miss Irene said, "Please, Maly, tell me what I have that you want, and I'll gladly give it to you." Maly placed her hand over her heart and replied, "I want what you have on the *inside* that makes you so kind to people like me."

The best part of what any of us has to give to another is what is on the inside. But somehow we have gotten the idea that we become better, more popular, more effective according to our outward appearance. So we spend endless hours trying to find the perfect make-up, the most becoming hair style, the most flattering clothing. No doubt, some of us could use a little help, but the best cosmetic might be an active mind and a loving heart.

An ancient proverb states, "If you have two loaves of bread, sell one and, with the money you obtain, go and buy hyacinths to feed your soul." The hyacinth plant, which grows from a small bulb, remains dormant for many months. Then in springtime a spike of small fragrant, bell-shaped flowers appears. The beauty and the aroma are worth the wait.

We each have immense potential—to love, to care, to create, to grow, to share. But it takes time apart to know the God who sustains us and to nourish the beauty that is within. We can only become as strong and as pure as we allow God to make us.

> *Speak, Lord in the stillness*
> *While I wait on Thee;*
> *Hushed my heart to listen*
> *in expectancy.*

Author Unknown

Prayer: Give us grace, O God, to seek the silent places and sit in your presence apart from the clamor of the world. Help us to rid our lives of the things that cloud our vision; grant us the insight to see what is important. Make and keep us pure within. Amen.

Seek Us When We Go Astray

"For thus says the Lord God: Behold, I, I myself will search for my sheep, and will seek them out. As a shepherd seeks out his flock when some of his sheep have been scattered abroad, so will I seek out my sheep . . .

Ezekiel 34:11-12

We are thine; do thou befriend us;
Be the guardian of our way;
Keep thy flock; from sin defend us;
Seek us when we go astray.
Blessed Jesus, blessed Jesus,
Hear thy children when we pray.
blessed Jesus, blessed Jesus,
hear thy children when we pray.

Savior, Like a Shepherd Lead Us
Dorothy A. Thrupp

Have you ever watched a shepherd tend his sheep? Some years ago I watched a shepherd in the Holy Land working with his flock. While I rode along the highway in comfort with friends, the shepherd trudged along beneath the heat of the sun with his sheep. Over the rocky, dusty terrain through brambles and scrub, he stayed with them. When the sheep nibbled themselves into undesirable places, the shepherd followed and gently nudged them back to safety.

I shared this experience with a farmer friend while he was preparing to shear some of his sheep. Our conversation drifted to their habits. "Sheep do not deliberately go astray," he commented. "They get lost simply by nibbling away at the grass, and never looking up."

That can be true of many of us as well. God permits us to wander freely along our own pathway. Like sheep, we often spend our time on what is immediately before us giving little attention to what lies beyond. Then suddenly we realize we are on unfamiliar ground unable to locate or recognize a familiar landmark. It is then that we truly need a shepherd.

How many times have we silently cried out, "O God, help me. Please show me that you care." We wait for a signal that he has heard our plea. Then the telephone rings. Someone from whom we haven't heard in a long, long time responds to our weak "hello" by saying, "I was thinking about you and . . ." God seeks us through a friend.

At other times he may seek us through the stranger who moves in next door or an event such as a memorial service or concert. Perhaps he may remind us of his presence through an object of beauty like the shell that washes up on shore, stopping right at our feet. Small events, perhaps, but all can serve to remind us of a caring shepherd who walks with us in ways we have yet to recognize.

Seek Us When We Go Astray

We do have to be ready to respond to his gentle nudging. We have to acknowledge the need for a shepherd and be willing to follow as he guides us back to safety. Unlike sheep, we follow intelligently, listening with discernment to his call, and responding gratefully to his loving care.

Prayer: O God, shepherd of our lives, we acknowledge that we often go astray like lost sheep. We are thine; do thou befriend us; be the guardian of our way. Amen.

Then the Hand of Jesus Touched Me

And he stretched out his hand and touched him . . .

Luke 5:13

Shackled by a heavy burden,
'neath a load of guilt and shame,
then the hand of Jesus touched me,
and now I am no longer the same.

He Touched Me
William J. Gaither

An old legend says that three young ladies once disputed about their hands, as to whose were the most beautiful. One of them dipped her hand in the pure stream, another picked berries until her fingers were pink, and the third gathered flowers whose fragrance clung to her hands. An old, haggard woman passed by and asked for assistance, but all refused her. Another young woman, plain and with no claim to beauty of hand, satisfied her need. The old woman then said, "It is not the hand that is washed in the brook, nor the hand tinted with red, nor the hand garlanded and perfumed with flowers that is most beautiful, but the hand that reaches out and touches those in need." As she spoke, her wrinkles were gone, her staff was thrown away, and she stood there—an angel from heaven. This is only a legend, but its judgment is true.

Visiting a leper colony could be an unpleasant and disturbing experience. All the things one has heard about the disease—the eating away of parts of the body, the disfigurement and unpleasant odor that follow, the isolation and the need to avoid contact—could instill fear and reservation in one's mind. But a visit to the McKean Rehabilitation Institute in Chiang Mai, Thailand, some years ago dispelled my fears. I found people being lovingly cared for by the Church, and I was able to join some of the patients as they gathered at mealtime and for worship. I will never forget visiting the physical therapy room where I saw individuals with no feet massaging the fingers and hands of fellow lepers who had recently had surgery. The untouchables were being touched by caring hands.

Recent outbreaks of contagious diseases and the fear of being accused of showing too much affection has regrettably caused many persons to refrain from touching others. In a church newsletter, Dr. Gina Rhea raises some interesting questions.

> Have you ever shaken hands with someone over the
> phone?
> Has anyone ever hugged your neck from the other
> side of the room?
> Have you ever heard someone whisper in your ear

from twenty feet away?
Have you ever seen a doctor set a broken arm from
across the street?

Of course not! Intimacy is needed for a few things. Obviously, Jesus thought so, too. The blind man who received his sight, the woman who was healed, and the children who were blessed all knew the value of his touch.

His presence becomes real in today's world through the warm touch of a loving and caring hand. It can have transforming results. How good it feels when one is ill to have a cool hand rubbed across the forehead. How comforting is the touch of a mother to a disturbed child. How consoling is the hand placed on one's shoulder as he awaits the return of a loved one from surgery or grieves over the loss of a friend. How encouraging is the handclasp when one is greeted by a friend or welcomed by a stranger.

Prayer: Touch our hands, O God, that our touch may bring strength to others. Amen.

His Love Shall Spread from Shore to Shore

The Mighty One, God the LORD,
speaks and summons the earth
from the rising of the sun to its setting.
Psalm 50:1

Jesus shall reign
where'er the sun
does its successive journeys run;
his love shall spread from shore to shore
till moons shall wax
and wane no more.

Jesus Shall Reign Where'er the Sun
Isaac Watts

Each year on the first Friday in March, women from all over the world join in celebration of their faith as they unite in World Day of Prayer. This circle of prayer, begun in 1887, begins with the rising of the sun on the Pacific island of Tonga, and for the next twenty-four hours women from every continent and island join in the great chain for "informed prayer and prayerful action."

Most of us know little about this once-pagan island or its strong link to the hymn "Jesus Shall Reign," for which Isaac Watts wrote the words in 1719.

In 1821 the natives of Fiji, where many of the inhabitants had become Christian, were terrified by the sight of a Tonga war-canoe rapidly approaching the shore. Its occupants were not coming to kill but—of all things in the world—to buy a Bible, relates W. J. Limmer in his book *Great Hymns and Their Stories.*

The people of Tonga had heard of the white man's religion and wanted to know about it. Although members of an expedition sent sometime earlier never returned to the island, a second canoe was sent across the 250 miles of open sea, its occupants seeking a copy of the Christian's book. It never occurred to them that it would be useless since none of them could read.

When the second canoe returned, however, a Bible and a missionary were on board. The result was a mass Christian movement led by the native monarch, King George. The movement was so successful that on Whitsunday/Pentecost, 1862, under the branches of the banyan trees, more than a thousand natives of Tonga, Fiji, and the Samoa islands gathered, and King George, surrounded by his chiefs and warriors, formally declared the islands to be Christian. He gave the people a new constitution, exchanging a heathen government for a Christian one. The whole multitude broke into song, singing the hymn which had been translated into the Tongan language:

His Love Shall Spread from Shore to Shore

To Christ shall endless prayer be made,
and endless praises crown his head;
his name like sweet perfume shall rise
with every morning sacrifice.

While it may be difficult to place a value on just one Bible or the blessings that can result from the message of just one individual, let us remember that whenever and wherever we pray, many others have or will gather—some out of doors, others in schools, hospitals, places of business, some in mud huts or great cathedrals—but all will be uniting in prayer.

Through prayer we extend our influence far beyond the range of our own voices. As we pray, alone or in the company of others, we allow the love of God to flow from our lives into the lives of others.

Prayer: We thank you, O Lord, for the wonderful privilege of prayer that allows us to be freed from our own selfishness. Magnify our concern for all people everywhere. Reign in our lives as we join with others around the world in proclaiming your love from shore to shore. Amen.

Fill Me with Life Anew

. . . then the LORD *God formed man of dust from the ground, and breathed into his nostrils the breath of life; and man became a living being.*
Genesis 2:7

Breathe on me, Breath of God,
fill me with life anew,
that I may love
what thou dost love,
and do what thou wouldst do.

Breathe on Me, Breath of God
Edwin Hatch

One wintry morning a neighbor drove past a group of school children hovered close together waiting for the bus. She noticed that they were amusing themselves by blowing their breath into the air while they waited. Perhaps they were pretending they were blowing smoke as children are sometimes prone to do. At any rate, they appeared to enjoy watching their breath ebb and flow in front of them.

Fill Me with Life Anew

Driving on down the highway, she tried to catch their spirit by blowing her breath into the air only to have the windshield fog over. She ceased that activity in a hurry, but she began to think about how precious breath and breathing are and how much we take them for granted. The words to the familiar hymn "Breathe on Me, Breath of God" kept flowing in and out of her mind all day as she went about her work.

We hear little, if anything, about the breath of God these days. Perhaps it is because we cannot see it. We only feel it! Just as there is something of the sun in every ray of light, there is something of the breath of God in every one of us. When Jesus came to his disciples following the resurrection "*. . . and stood among them and said to them, 'Peace be with you,'*" they were no doubt startled. "*. . . he showed them his hands and his side. Then the disciples were glad when they saw the Lord.*"

Jesus said to them again, "*Peace be with you. As the father has sent me, even so I send you.*" And when he had said this, "*He breathed on them.*" (John 20:19-22) He gave them something of his ways and mind and nature—his own spirit. He filled them with life anew.

An elderly Sunday school teacher illustrated this best when she said to her class one morning, "With each breath I whisper 'I adore thee.' I am strong when he is by my side. I want you to know him, too."

God is still breathing on us the breath of life. He can fill us with life anew, but first we must recognize his presence within and around us.

O Breath of Love, come, breathe within us,
renewing thought and will and heart.
Come, love of Christ, afresh to win us;
revive your church in every part.

Bessie Porter Head

Prayer: O Lord, you are the author of life. You have given us breath to praise you and words to proclaim your abiding love. Help us to walk day by day in a fresh awareness of your presence. Amen.

He Lives Within My Heart

And he said to them, "Do not be amazed; you seek Jesus of Nazareth, who was crucified. He has risen, he is not here; see the place where they laid him.
Mark 16:6

He lives, he lives,
Christ Jesus lives today!
He walks with me and talks with me
along life's narrow way.
He lives, he lives,
salvation to impart!
You ask me how I know he lives?
He lives within my heart.

He Lives!
Thomas O. Chisolm

Not long ago I decided that I needed to get busy completing a task I'd put off for years—organizing (and maybe discarding) those pictures that I had been accumulating but had never put in an album. What I thought would be an easy task has become a journey down memory lane. There are many pictures of family members and friends who are now deceased or with whom I have lost contact. As I examine each photo, trying to remember when and where it was taken and who I see portrayed, sometimes I feel joy and excitement, sometimes sadness and loss.

There are even some faded black-and-white photos taken years ago as we prepared for a sunrise service at church. There was the garden scene with the stone rolled away and two friends dressed as angels. What memories!

When I begin to feel that too many memories are crowding in, I move on to the next task of the day, but those persons and the love we shared continue to linger and live within my heart.

Each year as the Lenten and Easter seasons approach, theologians and secularists alike seem to delight in raising questions about what really happened on that first Easter morning. There is sometimes confusion about who went to the tomb, where Jesus was seen, and who saw him. The early disciples were not so concerned with all the specifics. They knew that while Jesus had been with them, he had compassion for the poor; he healed the sick; he made lonely people feel needed and important. And most of all, they felt his living presence within their lives.

Today we often have to rely on symbols to lift our spirits and jog our memories. The butterfly is one such symbol. Artists capture butterflies' beauty in stained glass. Others create them using gold beads and pearls, proudly displaying them during the Advent and Christmas seasons. Jewelers create beautiful pins that are sometimes worn on the shoulder for all to see. With wings arched upward, butterflies symbolize the resurrection and his presence in the world of today.

Easter cannot be proven, only experienced. The power of Easter comes whenever and wherever we remember and feel his living presence in our lives. Jesus lives wherever there is faith to believe he is alive. "If he lives, then he must live within our hearts," stated the Reverend Rollin C. Hill. "And He must be proclaimed as King of Kings and Lord of Lords not only in the past but NOW."

Prayer: O Living Lord, enter into our hearts this day with all your risen power. May we not only feel your presence but witness your love at work in the world within us and through us. Amen.

I Am the Clay

Yet, O Lord, thou art our Father;
we are the clay, and thou art our potter;
we are all the work of thy hand.
                    Isaiah 64:8

Have thine own way, Lord!
Have thine own way!
Thou art the potter; I am the clay.
Mold me and make me after thy will,
while I am waiting, yielded and still.

Have Thine Own Way, Lord!
Adelaide A. Pollard

I find it fascinating to watch a potter working at his wheel. On vacations I seek out the potter's house in the area so I can watch the artist as he takes a lump of clay and carefully works it with his hands, preparing to throw it onto the wheel. I am told that the potter's serious work really begins as he throws the clay onto the wheel and begins the act of centering. The clay becomes a spinning, unwobbling pivot that will then be free to take on whatever shape the potter chooses.

Mary Caroline Richards in *Alive Now*, an Upper Room publication, states, "It is difficult, if not impossible for a potter to force his clay into the center simply by exerted pressure. In order to take its new shape, the clay has to move . . . Once it has become centered, it will remain so unless there is a flaw in the clay or unless it is knocked off center."

Today we are confident that the answers to all our problems lie within ourselves, if only we could find them. Or, at the other extreme, we are so despondent that we cannot see beyond ourselves to God. Is not our need to be broken and centered once again on the potter's wheel, there to have our lives re-fashioned according to his will?

"Behold, like the clay in the potter's hand, so are you in my hand," writes Jeremiah. (Jeremiah 18:6) Just as a piece of canvas does not become a painting until it has made contact with the one who creates it, so we do not become what God wants us to be until we have allowed ourselves to yield under his hands. We must remember that it is a frightening thing for us as clay to fall into the hands of the living God. But it is much more frightening to fall out of his hands.

When our lives wobble and we stumble, perhaps we have traveled too far from the center of our own creation. It is then that we need to allow ourselves to return to the Master's hands.

We are, after all, like lumps of clay.
There are brittle pieces, hard pieces,

BLESSED ASSURANCE

We have little shape or beauty.
But we need not despair. If we are clay,
let us remember, that there is a Potter
and His Wheel.

Peter Marshall

Prayer: Have thine own way Lord; have thine own way!
Thou art the potter; I am the clay. Mold me and make me,
after thy will. While I am waiting, yielded and still. Amen.

In Seasons of Distress and Grief

Cast all your anxieties on him, for he cares about you.
1 Peter 5:7

Sweet hour of prayer! Sweet hour of prayer!
that calls me from a world of care,
and bids me at my Father's throne
make all my wants and wishes known.
In seasons of distress and grief,
my soul has often found relief,
and oft escaped the tempter's snare
by thy return, sweet hour of prayer!

Sweet Hour of Prayer!
William Walford

Paul in his letter to "the saints who are at Philippi" shared with them that he had suffered the loss of all things. Then he affirms:
Brethren, I do not consider that I have made it on my own; but one thing I do, forgetting what lies behind,

*and straining forward to what lies ahead, I press on
toward the goal for the prize of the upward call of
God in Christ Jesus.*

Philippians 3:13, 14

Everyone who lives will pass through periods of comfort and joy and periods of distress and sadness. At some time or other, we will all know some time of suffering, heartbreak, or disappointment. We will all fail and make mistakes. Most of us will experience depression, which may range all the way from a normal reaction to grief or a discouraging situation to a neurotic or severe depression that must be treated by a physician. But Paul urges us not to allow these heartaches, sorrows, and disappointments to break us.

There is a certain kind of pine called the limber pine found in the mountains of the western United States. I have been told that its branches can literally be tied into knots. Its flexibility and resiliency make this possible. When you untie the knots, the branches assume their original shape. Such trees ride out the winds and storms that destroy other trees by bending with the wind, but they spring erect after the storm has passed. Christ does not and will not remove life's difficulties, but he does give us help in facing them. Our faith and trust in him will enable us to pass through seasons of distress and grief and spring back after the storm has passed.

It will be up to us to take the first step in rising above disturbing experiences. When we do, we will find God waiting to comfort, to heal, and to give to us the promise of renewed joy. God is for us! Life is not empty, and we are not alone. In the loneliest situation or experience there are two of us.

> *My God and I go in the field together.*
> *We walk and talk as good friends should*
> *and do*

. . . .

> *This earth will pass, and with it common trifles*
> *But God and I will go unendingly.*
>   Austris A. Wihtol

Prayer: O God, direct us into those ways of devotion that will give us lives strong enough to meet life's hardest trials without breaking. Help us to know that again and again joy returns to life. Amen.

Take Away Our Love of Sinning

I do not understand my own actions. For I do not
do what I want, but I do the very thing I hate . . .
For I do not do the good I want, but the evil I do
not want is what I do.
Romans 7:15, 19

Breathe, O breathe thy loving Spirit
into every troubled breast;
let us all in thee inherit,
let us find thy promised rest;
take away our love of sinning;
alpha and omega be;
end of faith, as its beginning,
set our hearts at liberty.

Love Divine, All Loves Excelling
Charles Wesley

*T*he Adventures of Huckleberry Finn had nearly
escaped my memory when my grandsons asked
me to take them to the movie. As I observed
Huck's escapades, I found that I really had forgotten how

sly he really was. Huckleberry seemed to go to great lengths to avoid responsibility. He had an aversion to school and hard work. He would rather fish.

We probably wouldn't classify Huck's misadventures as sins but perhaps just as a part of growing up. But doesn't it always seem more exciting to do what we are advised not to do even if we have already grown up? For instance, a sign at the counter of a local drugstore read, "Ring the bell ONLY once if you need assistance." Somehow it was a real temptation not to hit it several times just because the sign said not to.

We customarily regard sin as wrongdoing, breaking the law of God, enticement, or evil. If these concepts are corthe love of sinning has been around for a long, long time. Clergy of all denominations and faiths get a lot of advice from persons both within and outside their immediate congregations. A recent cartoon depicted "the Reverend" in the doorway greeting persons as they exited the morning worship service. As one of the faithful approached, she was overheard imparting a little advice. "Your sermon on sin was a bit weak," she stated. "I thought you might want to hire a special consultant."

Perhaps that wouldn't be such a bad idea. We tend to include such things as stealing, lying, cruelty, and murder as sins. But we often stop short of including gossip, slander, greed, pettiness, criticism, jealousy, and anger. We would prefer to consider them minor flaws. A consultant might remind us that even committing the lesser sins can be dangerous. They can weaken our resolve and make it easier for us to commit the more serious offenses.

One of the most precious gifts we have is the ability to make choices and direct our own lives. It may be more troublesome to do right, but in the end it will not only prove to be good for us but beneficial to those around us. Nothing is so contagious as our example, be it for evil or for good.

Prayer: Cleanse us, O Lord, from our indifferent attitude, our mean ambitions, our sinful lusts, that we may be ready for your transforming love. Grant us honesty in confronting and confessing our sins and humility in seeking forgiveness. Give us the courage to deal with our own sins before we condemn those of our neighbor. Take away our love of sinning; set our hearts at liberty. Amen.

The Light of His Smile

I smiled on them when they had no
* confidence;*
and the light of my countenance
* they did not cast down.*
                    Job 29:24

Living for Jesus through earth's little while,
my dearest treasure—the light of his smile;
seeking the lost ones he died to redeem,
bringing the weary to find rest in him.
      O Jesus, Lord and Savior,
      I give myself to thee . . .
my life I give, henceforth to live,
      O Christ, for thee alone.

Living for Jesus
Thomas O. Chisolm

A friend related how she waited nervously in the dentist's chair for Dr. Pryor to enter the room. The few minutes' delay began to seem like hours as she sat entertaining herself by reading every chart on the wall. She soon noticed a picture of a kitten nestled quietly and solemnly in some shrubbery. The inscription above it was so small that she had to get out of the chair and move closer to read it. "If you see someone without a smile on his face, give him one of yours," it said. She settled back in the chair with renewed calmness and smiled as she recalled a verse from Proverbs, *"A merry heart doeth good like a medicine."* (Proverbs 17:22)

"How do you measure the value of a smile? It costs nothing, but creates much good. It enriches those who receive it without impoverishing those who give it away. It happens in a flash, but the memory of it can last forever. No one is so rich that he can get along without it; no one is too poor to feel rich when receiving it. It creates happiness in the home, fosters goodwill in business, and is the countersign of friends. It is rest to the weary, daylight to the discouraged, sunshine to the sad, and nature's best antidote for trouble. Yet it cannot be bought, begged, borrowed or stolen, for it is something of no earthly good to anybody until it is given away willingly."

While the author of these words remains anonymous, the words tell us of an inner peace and strength.

"We live in a world," wrote British novelist and essayist Aldous Huxley, "which is full of misery and ignorance, and the plain duty of each and all of us is to try to make the little corner he can influence somewhat less miserable and somewhat less ignorant than it was before he entered it."

This can be done if we remember to carry a smile with us wherever we go. A friendly smile might be the greatest gift we can give to someone who looks to us for inspiration, courage, or comfort. And it doesn't do any harm to smile and say "Good morning," even if it is raining.

Perhaps the patient who gave the picture of the kitten to the dentist as a Christmas gift knew that others would sit in that same chair and need to be smiled upon.

Prayer: O Lord, our smiles don't always come easily. We often allow ourselves to become bogged down by the weight of daily activity and fail to permit the sunshine of joy to find its way into our lives. Strengthen us that we may live closer to you and thus be able to share the light of your smile with others. Amen.

My Listening Ears

Let me hear what God the LORD will speak,
for he will speak peace to his people,
to his saints, to those who turn to him in their hearts.
Psalm 85:8

This is my Father's world,
and to my listening ears,
all nature sings and round me rings
the music of the spheres.
This is my Father's world;
I rest me in the thought
of rocks and trees, of skies and seas;
God's hands the wonders wrought.

This Is My Father's World
Maltbie D. Babcock

L istening is difficult in these days, amid the jangling phones, clattering computers and fax machines, racing engines, screeching tires, blaring sirens, radios, televisions, alarm clocks, video games, gossiping voices, children's cries and laughter—all the noise of everyday living. But listen we must! Like musicians whose trained ears hear both the harmony and the discord, we need to cultivate the art of listening so that we can hear both the notes of joy and the calls for help.

While walking in an area mall, I heard a child crying. When I looked around to see what was wrong, I saw just behind me a mother walking with a young child in tow. The child seemed to be turning her tears on and off at will. As they passed me, I overheard the little one say, "Mommy, pick me up. Can't you hear me crying?" The mother obviously heard but wasn't listening.

Listening to someone means opening every hearing channel of our body and listening not only with our ears but also with our eyes, mind, and feelings.

The ability to give one's complete attention to another person is a great gift that comes when we have learned to hear not only words but also meanings. For example, one of the certainties of going on a cruise is that sometime early in the voyage the passengers will be drilled in disembarkation procedures should difficulties arise while the vessel is at sea. Everyone is instructed to report to a designated location at a certain time with life jacket in hand. There a crew member actually instructs and rehearses with the passengers the donning of the life jacket and leads them to the deck where the emergency lifeboats are located. Passengers listen with every hearing channel their bodies can muster. Life depends on it!

Our lives as Christians also depend on our willingness to listen for "the still, small voice of God." God needs listeners—those whose ears are attuned to hear and who are alert to ways in which they can be used to reconcile people to one another and to him. There is no limit to what God can do through us if we are listening.

> *In the rustling grass I hear God pass,*
> *who speaks to me everywhere.*

The question is, "Am I listening?"

> *Be still and know*
> *That God is in his world.*
> *God speaks, but none may hear*
> *That voice except he have*
> *The listening ear.*
> Author Unknown

Prayer: O Lord, give us the grace of listening. Amid the noise and confusion of each day, enable us not only to listen and hear the hurts and joys of those around us but also to respond with a listening heart. Amen.

Forbid It, Lord,
That I Should Boast

*"Beware of practicing your piety before men in order
to be seen by them; for then you will have no reward
from your Father who is in heaven.*
Matthew 6:1

Forbid it, Lord, that I should boast,
save in the death of Christ, my God;
all the vain things that charm me most
I sacrifice them to his blood.

When I Survey the Wondrous Cross
Isaac Watts

A small group of friends gather occasionally for lunch at their favorite Chinese restaurant. They enjoy the atmosphere, fellowship, and food as well as the sharing that comes when the bowl of fortune cookies is placed on the table. The maxims they contain originate in what might be called a "Chinese Philosophy Factory." These fortune slips are printed on large sheets of paper, separated, and mixed with others. Then they are inserted into hot, pliable wafers that are folded and shaped in a mold around the slip of paper, then cooled and wrapped. Sometime later, they arrive at tables to be opened, shared, and often debated. It's amazing how varied and seemingly right on target these words of wisdom can be.

> "The time to be happy is now."
> "The best way to stop a bad habit is never
> to begin it."
> "Difficulties are a challenge, not a barrier."

Occasionally, the axioms promise good fortune: "You will receive the blessing of a relative," or "Your long-awaited ship will soon anchor."

They also can be humbling:

"If you wish to succeed, consult three old people."

"They can do least who boast loudest."

In Romans 12, Paul sends some rather good words of wisdom to those gathered in Rome and in towns and cities everywhere:

> *Having gifts that differ, let us use them.* (v.3)
> *Let love be genuine; bless those who persecute you.*
>   (v.9)
> *Do not think of yourself more highly than you*
>   *ought.* (v.12)
> *Beware of practicing your piety.* (v.12)
> *Let him who boasts, boast in the Lord.* (v.16)

Forbid It, Lord, That I Should Boast

Paul did not mean we should never think highly of ourselves or even be a little pleased when we do something that is especially nice. He is simply saying to us that we should be careful lest we become conceited, lest we do too much bragging.

There is an old story about the second man in an Oriental kingdom who carried a small chest with him wherever he went. The people were very curious about its contents. Finally, one person gathered up enough courage to ask what His Highness protected in the chest. The ruler opened the chest and revealed its contents—the common clothing of a working man. The questioner was shocked. The ruler explained, "I was a common working man when our sovereign king chose me for this royal position. If I am ever tempted to boast, I correct it by looking at these things and saying to myself, 'Remember what you once were.'"

God is not impressed with our status or symbols of power. He is concerned only with the attitude and spirit of the heart.

Prayer: You know us, O God, better than anyone else. Teach us to keep our lives in proper balance. Search us and know our hearts; bend our pride to your control. Amen.

For the Joy of Human Love

For the joy of human love,
brother, sister, parent, child,
friends on earth, and friends above,
for all gentle thoughts and mild,
Lord of all, to thee we raise
this our hymn of grateful praise.

For the Beauty of the Earth
Folliot S. Pierpoint

A mother discovered her young son carefully alter-
nating bites of his ice cream cone between himself
and his puppy. Rather unsympathetically, she asked
why he was feeding such good food to his dog. The gleeful
reply was, "It's more funner when there's two."

Few of us prefer being alone or doing things alone.
Most of us enjoy the company and friendship of others.

Someone has likened humans to plants that need certain elements for their development. We all need the soft, warm earth of love for nourishment, the rain of kindness, and the sun of encouragement. All of us need others—others in whom we can become interested, show concern, and with whom we can build bridges of friendship.

In the story of the creation found in the second chapter of Genesis, the Lord God said, *"It is not good that the man should be alone; I will make him a helper fit for him."* (Genesis 2:18)

So he formed the beasts of the field and every bird of the air. They were all given names, but there was not found a helper fit for the man. So God created woman. The animals would be helpers, but God saw the need for human love.

Some years ago the sitcom *Golden Girls* provided interesting, light-hearted television viewing on Saturday nights. The story line revolved around four women who, for one reason or another, shared a house in Miami, Florida. The specifics of the episodes have escaped my memory but the theme song still surfaces in my mind—"Thank You For Being a Friend."

Thank you for being a friend. To love and be loved! These are essential human needs. We are all dependent upon someone else. Others depend on us as well. Take one violin from the orchestra, and the music is not the same. God provides us with opportunities for friendship. He provides us people with whom to work, with whom to live. He provides people whom we can help and who can help us. Different as we are, with different backgrounds defining our views, we all need one another. But love and friendship are not learned until they are practiced.

Let us not wait until someone shows love to us to share our tokens of love—a smile, a compliment, a kind word, a bouquet of flowers, an unexpected visit, a telephone call, an ice cream cone. Sometimes we will be prone to strike out on our own like the Prodigal Son, wishing to divorce ourselves from family and friends. Isolation at times will seem preferable to sharing our lives with others. When that happens, let us remember that the Prodigal Son came home for the joy of human love.

Prayer: Loving and gracious Lord, we pray for human companionship, for persons with whom we can be friends. Help us to support and understand one another. We are grateful that you reveal your love to us through the kindness of others. Amen.

Help Us Thy Name to Sing

O sing to the Lord a new song . . .
Declare his glory among the nations,
  his marvelous works among all the peoples!

Psalm 96:1, 3

Come, thou almighty King,
help us thy name to sing;
help us to praise:
one God, all glorious,
o'er all victorious,
come, and reign over us,
ancient of days.

Come, Thou Almighty King
Anonymous

Many of us cannot help but admire the meaning-ful lyrics of the late Oscar Hammerstein. They define an attitude toward life anyone might find helpful. He once said that he could not write a song with-out hope in it. He knew, as we all do, that life is not all beautiful. There is ugliness we must all be aware of and must work as hard as we can to change. But we cannot let the unpleasant events in life cause us to lose hope. Isaiah challenged us to move beyond despair when he wrote:

> *Get you up to a high mountain,*
> *O Zion, herald of good tidings;*
> *lift up your voice with strength,*
> *O Jerusalem, herald of good tidings,*
> *lift it up, fear not . . .*
>
> Isaiah 40:9

A group of children gathered around the minister at the front of the sanctuary for their weekly mini-sermon. After they had greeted each other and had settled enough to listen, the minister began by asking the active preschoolers if they knew how we talk with God. Nathan quickly responded in a voice loud enough for everyone to hear, "Nope! And I won't know unless you tell me." Nathan and others like him, whether young or not so young, will never know the wonders of God's love unless we tell them. From the first century onward, Christian experience has been spread by means of personal witness and testimony. It is by telling the "good news" that the gospel of hope is spread.

"The word *gospel* literally comes from the Greek word *evangelion* which is the root of our word *evangel*, *evangelize* and *evangelist*," stated Paul A. Crow, Jr. "The word in the first appearance in English was *god-spell* meaning good tidings. This was later shortened to *Godspel*, that is, God's story, and eventually became '*Gospel*.'"

Help Us Thy Name to Sing

As followers of Jesus, we share the good tidings of hope by passing them on to others. Some of us will share them through the spoken word. Others of us, even if not musically inclined, may sing of his glorious love. Monita Crane once said, "You don't have to know how to sing. It's feeling as though you want to that makes the day successful." How true this is. Whether we praise his name through the spoken word or the melody of a song, we must always share his name through our acts and attitudes as we live lives filled with hope.

Prayer: Lord, help us to share your wondrous story. May we continue to sing until the whole world has learned of your love and forgiveness. Amen.

In Love God Made Them All

O LORD, how manifold are thy works!
In wisdom hast thou made them all.
Psalm 104:24

Each little flower that opens,
each little bird that sings,
God made their glowing colors,
and made their tiny wings.
All things bright and beautiful,
all creatures great and small,
all things wise and wonderful,
in love God made them all.

All Things Bright and Beautiful
Cecil F. Alexander

We often bemoan the weeds that crop up in our yards and gardens. Dandelions, in particular, are a source of irritation. But to a young Israeli girl they represented beauty. Several churches in a small town in southwest Virginia served as hosts for a group of European students. The town's mayor made their visit unforgettable by declaring each student an honorary citizen. When Hannah's name was called and she was given her certificate, she presented Mayor Edens with a small bouquet of dandelions she had picked from the lawn outside the municipal building. The mayor graciously accepted the bouquet and later commented, "She has seen the hidden beauty in a common plant which I failed to see. I'll never think of dandelions as weeds again."

"Never lose an opportunity of seeing anything that is beautiful; for beauty is God's handwriting—a wayside sacrament," wrote Ralph Waldo Emerson. "Welcome it in every fair face, in every fair sky, in every fair flower, and thank God for it as a cup of blessing."

The ancient Hebrew psalmist did not know the wonderful facts of our universe as we know them today. Nevertheless, in the presence of such grandeur and beauty as he could see, he exclaimed:

When I look at thy heavens, the work of thy fingers,
the moon and the stars which thou hast established;
what is man that thou art mindful of him,
and the son of man that thou dost care for him?
Psalm 8:3, 4

There is a shrub in Bermuda called "match me if you can." During a bus tour of the island, the driver pointed out the plant to a group of tourists. "It was given that name," he said, "because no two leaves are ever alike." One curious visitor asked if there would be a convenient spot to stop so she could view the shrub more closely. Shortly thereafter, the driver pulled the bus over to the side of the road and invited anyone who wished to reach out the window and gather a few leaves. After careful examination, the skeptics were convinced that the leaves could not be matched, for no two were alike.

God loans us the wealth and beauty of the universe to care for and enjoy. Let us not become so involved in every-day living that we fail to see the miraculous gifts of his creation, including the gift of our lives. No two of us are alike.

Prayer: Thank you, O God, for being so extravagant with beauty. Help us to see and know it as your handiwork. May our gratitude be reflected in our daily living. Help us to remember whenever we see a flower, a blade of grass, a tree, a leaf, the ocean, a shell washed upon the beach, a butterfly, or anything of beauty in all of creation that you, the Lord God, made them all. Amen.

Make My Heart Anew

A glad heart makes a cheerful countenance.
Proverbs 15:13

God, who touches earth with beauty,
make my heart anew.
With your Spirit recreate me
pure and strong and true.

God, Who Touchest Earth with Beauty
Mary S. Edgar

Ernest Nesbit, a scientist, spent his life learning about plants and seeds. He learned early to plant the seeds carefully in the right kinds of soil, to provide the proper nourishment, and to be patient as growth took place. One day a friend came to visit him and found him sitting in front of a plant, just looking at it. "What do you see that's so interesting?" the friend asked. "Oh, I'm watching God at work," he replied.

Nesbit had learned well that once the seed was planted it must be nourished in order to germinate and produce a mature plant. So it is with us. For some, the seed was planted years ago, perhaps when we were young. For others, it may have been planted in later life but never properly nourished. Perhaps it has been lying dormant for many years as we struggled with earning a living and caring for a family. When tempers flared or discord arose, we were quick to excuse our behavior and ready to blame the circumstances.

"Up to the time of the coming of the Christian faith," wrote J. B. Phillips in *Good News,* "religion had been almost entirely a matter of obeying the laws of an 'external' God. The new thing which Christ brought into being was that God himself, by his Spirit, was entering into men's hearts, and transforming them from the inside."

The significant factors that could change us—from gloom to joy, from despair to hope, from doubt to faith, from ordinary to lovely— lie within us. We may not see it, but God has designed beauty and loveliness for every life.

Perhaps it will be in the silence that we find the direction that gives meaning to our lives. God says to each of us, "If you would just empty your vessel, I will fill it. Empty your mind of all that limits your loveliness, nourish your heart and mind with thoughts that heal and cleanse." Job's declaration: *"There was silence, then I heard a voice,"* (Job 4:16) speaks a reminder to our busy lives. Silence is for hearing the voice of God and allowing him to work within us. May we never forget that each of us is a work of art, signed by God's own hands.

Prayer: Grant us the patience, O Lord, to stop and listen for your guidance in our lives. Amen.

Take It to the Lord in Prayer

Trust in the LORD *with all your heart,*
and do not rely on your own insight.
Proverbs 3:5

Have we trials and temptations?
Is there trouble anywhere?
We should never be discouraged;
take it to the Lord in prayer!
Can we find a friend so faithful,
who will all our sorrows share?
Jesus knows our every weakness;
take it to the Lord in prayer.

What a Friend We Have in Jesus
Joseph Scriven

Vance Havner tells about a textile factory with a sign over the machines that read: "When threads get tangled, send for the foreman." One day a workman got his threads tangled and tried desperately to untangle them himself. He was making a worse mess when the foreman came along and asked, "Don't you see the sign?"

"Yes," was the reply, "but I am doing the best I can to take care of it myself." "Doing the best you can," came the answer, "always means sending for the foreman."

The best thing we can do when the threads of life become tangled is to take it to the Lord in prayer. We will pray most often when we hurt, when sickness, worry, depression, loss, and trials come our way. These prayers are sometimes what Urban G. Steinmetz called "back up against the wall" prayer. We have a problem and have tried everything. Finally, when things get really bad, we say, "Lord, I don't know what to do, but you do. I need your help." When our backs are against the wall, it is then that we call for the foreman.

Why do we wait until our lives become so fragile to seek God's help? Is it because he seems so far away from us, and we do not know how to get his attention? Perhaps we need to acknowledge that God is not a distant being waiting for our call. He is that friend already present, living within us, ready to comfort and guide. There is no time or place in which it is inappropriate to offer up a petition to God. We can pray walking down the street, while in a car, while waiting for the traffic light to change, or while working at something that does not require our full attention. God's presence is with us wherever we are. No appointment is necessary; no waiting in long lines. God is always there to meet us at our point of need. All we have to do is pause and ask for his guidance.

> *Lord, what a change within us one short hour*
> *Spent in thy presence will prevail to make:*

Take It to the Lord in Prayer

What heavy burdens from our bosom take.
What parched grounds refresh as with a shower!
We kneel, and all around us seems to lower;
We rise, and all, the distant and the near,
Stands forth in sunny outline brave and clear;
We kneel, how weak; we rise, how full of power!
Why, therefore, should we do ourselves this wrong,
Or others—that we are not always strong—
That we are ever overborne with care,
That we should ever weak or heartless be,
Anxious or troubled—when with us in prayer,
And joy and strength and courage are with Thee!

Archbishop Richard C. Trench

Prayer: Thank you, O Lord, for always being there for us.
Grant us the faith of a little child that in simple trust we can
acknowledge your presence in our lives. Amen.

Thy Mercies, How Tender

The steadfast love of the Lord *never ceases,*
his mercies never come to an end;
they are new every morning;
great is thy faithfulness.
Lamentations 3:22–23

Frail children of dust,
and feeble as frail;
in you do we trust,
nor find you to fail;
your mercies, how tender,
how firm to the end,
our Maker, Defender, Redeemer and Friend!

O Worship the King
Robert Grant

I t is difficult these days to drive anywhere without noticing the license plates on automobiles as they speed
down the highway. We even create games to keep grand-
children occupied as we travel. Sometimes we have a con-
test to see who can spot the most out-of-state license plates;

at other times we look for those specialized plates that are now in vogue.

A colleague, the Reverend Dr. Larry Hastings, shared his experience with license plates in a recent newsletter. He wrote that he was not having a very good day or even a very good week. While he drove his car down the interstate, the wheels in his head and heart were spinning jumbled thoughts about the approaching funeral eulogy, wedding homily, Sunday sermon, and newsletter column he had to prepare.

He was even suffering physical pain from emergency surgery to remove a tooth. Then he recalled the dentist who calmly began by saying, "This will only take a minute," while still yanking on his tooth fifty-five minutes later. "Every time I recalled the pressure," he wrote, "I noticed that I also pressed down a little harder on the accelerator. As I tried to pass the car in front of me, I glanced at its license plate. It said, 'IOGOD.' My car still traveled fifty-five miles per hour, but my soul came to a screeching halt. A warm gratitude pulsed through my body with each heartbeat. 'I owe God,'" he concluded.

We all owe God! Our lives are gifts, freely given to us, fresh and new each day. Every morning when we awaken from sleep and greet a new day, we live by God's mercy. Throughout this day, persons will surrender their lives to skilled surgeons, nurses, and technicians who labor to restore or at least improve their health. When it is all over, they are alive by God's mercy.

What is mercy? In the Bible the word *mercy* (often translated *loving-kindness*) refers to God's compassion toward us in times of weakness and misery. In common usage, mercy refers to more kindness than needed or kindness beyond what can be expected. A blind girl called it "the odor the flowers give when tramped upon," and Ralph Sockman defined it as "active compassion." However it is defined, the supreme quality of God is his mercy. Day after day, in faithfulness to us, he showers us with his loving-kindness.

> *Great is your faithfulness,*
> *O God my Father,*
> *Morning by morning new mercies I see.*

Thomas O. Chisholm

We owe God!

Prayer: Eternal God, whose tender mercies are ever ours to accept, grant us a new awareness of your presence throughout each day. Wherever we are, we pause to say thank you. Amen.

Give Me a Faithful Heart

Search me, O God, and know my heart!
Try me and know my thoughts!
Psalm 139:23

Give me a faithful heart,
guided by thee,
that each departing day
henceforth may see
some work of love begun,
some deed of kindness done,
some wanderer sought and won,
something for thee.

Savior, Thy Dying Love
Sylvanus Dryden Phelps

The story is told of a man who fed a beggar faithfully for some time. Eventually, the man himself was in great trouble, and it was necessary for someone to run an errand for him. He summoned the beggar and asked him to go. But the beggar replied, "Sir, I ask alms. I do not run errands."

What a picture of many of us! We ask blessings from God such as recovery from illness, a safe journey home, forgiveness for a wrong we have committed, and even material comforts. He never fails to guide us, yet we follow him with less than a faithful heart.

Faith is a gift from God. There is not one of us who does not have lots of it. It may be faith in good things or faith in wrong causes, but we have it. It is an integral part of our lives, and it exists at all levels, whether on the level of a four-leafed clover, or on the level of the astronauts who believed they could land on the moon. "Faith is not something we think. Rather we live it," writes Ted McEachern in his book *Being There for Others*. "Faith is not an idea, it is an event. As life and as events in our experience, faith happens in the world." It is an act of the heart. As a personal possession, we demonstrate faith in our lives and attitudes.

A traveler once crossed the desert led by an Arab guide who stopped to pray several times daily. Surprised, the traveler asked him why he prayed to someone he could not see. The Arab replied, "Last night when we slept, we heard a noise. How did you know camels passed by?" The traveler replied, "Because this morning I saw footprints." The wise Arab smiled, "And I've seen the marks of God in the fiery beauty of the sunset, in the cooling waters of the oasis, in the stars of heaven above. These were all made by one who leaves his footprints everywhere."

Faith implies belief. To own it, we must believe in someone or something greater than ourselves. Obedience is the best expression we can give to show our faithfulness.

Give Me a Faithful Heart

Prayer: O God of faithfulness, whose love abides throughout whatever life may bring, help us to place our trust in you. Fill our hearts with eagerness to bear witness to our faith, and forgive us when our love of things causes us to become unfaithful. Amen.

God Mend Thine Every Flaw

Blessed is the nation whose God is the LORD,
the people whom he has chosen as his heritage!
Psalm 33:12

O beautiful for patriot dream
that sees beyond the years
thine alabaster cities gleam,
undimmed by human tears!
America! America!
God mend thine every flaw,
confirm thy soul in self-control,
thy liberty in law.

O Beautiful for Spacious Skies
Katherine Lee Bates

Some twenty years ago, Dr. Louise Clark and I were in South Africa representing Church Women United in the United States on the *Christian Causeway to Africa*. We were enjoying Sunday breakfast in the home of an Anglican priest and his wife in Port Elizabeth. Just as we were completing our meal, their two children came running into the dining room. They stopped abruptly when they saw us, and one of them shouted, "They are pink ladies, not red Indians." Our outburst of laughter was followed by a brief discussion about Indians. We explained to them that there are Indians in the United States, but many look and dress just as we do. Only for special events do they paint their faces with war paint and dress in their native clothing, including feathered headpieces and moccasins.

This incident reminded me over the years of how we perceive and often misunderstand people both here at home and around the world. Our perception is often clouded by our knowledge, or lack thereof, of others' nationalities and cultures.

"It is one thing to recognize that some people are strangers to us—we know almost nothing about them, their clothing, their language; their habits may be totally different from ours; and it would be absurd to pretend we were buddies," writes David H. C. Read in his book, *An Expanding Faith*. "It is quite another thing to hate them for these differences, and hate can range all the way from bloody warfare to the polite social freeze."

Through our Christian faith we have come to believe in the perfect world God would have here on earth. But if we see clearly the world as it is today, we see a world of unrest and mistrust. Katherine Lee Bates also knew such a world when she penned the words: "America, America, God mend thine every flaw, Confirm thy soul in self-control, thy liberty in law."

A flaw is a crack, a slight defect, a blemish, or imperfection. If we were asked to make a list of our personal flaws and a separate list of our nation's flaws, would they be the same or close? Would they be flaws (sins) of disposition rather than flaws of the flesh? Would they include selfishness, greed, and lack of knowledge and understanding of others?

There are many references in the Gospels that condemn the flaws of the disposition more than the sins of the flesh.

Do not judge by appearances, but judge with right judgment.
John 7:24

Do nothing from selfishness or conceit, but in humility count others better than yourselves.
Philippians 2:3

It is perhaps too late for America to try to win anyone with words or giving alone. But we can win the world by example—by making our way of life as good and inclusive as we know how. When we are honest, we acknowledge that the problem is not the world but ourselves. It is our flaws that need mending. Anyone who wants to change the world must begin with himself or herself— the person over whom he or she has the most control.

Prayer: Forgive us, O Lord, when we wound others with careless words and deeds. May we continue to mend our flaws so that America may be worthy of the place of prestige it now has in the family of nations. Amen.

The Tempting Sounds I Hear

Don't let the world around you squeeze you into its own mold, but let God remold your minds from within.

Romans 12:2
J. B. Phillips
The New Testament in Modern English

O let me feel thee near me!
The world is ever near;
I see the sights that dazzle,
the tempting sounds I hear;
my foes are ever near me,
around me and within;
but, Jesus, draw thou nearer,
and shield my soul from sin.

O Jesus, I Have Promised
John E. Bode

An American was walking with an Asian friend down a busy street in one of our largest cities. "What? Can you can hear a cricket in all this traffic?" exclaimed the American to his friend. But a cricket it was, under a sidewalk grating. A few minutes later, the Asian friend marveled when suddenly several people ahead of them stopped. "What is it?" he asked. "Didn't you hear the coins drop from that man's pocket?" was the reply.

Somehow the sounds we hear and respond to most often are the sounds related to our desire for pleasure or gain. We hear the coin drop but not the chirp of the cricket. We hear the commercials advising us to rush out and purchase the newest gadget to help us lose weight. Those tempting sounds often sound like music to our ears. But we may fail to hear the public service announcement pleading for volunteers to deliver meals to the elderly.

According to legend, Ulysses, the shrewdest Greek leader in the Trojan War, was tempted by the beautiful voices of the Sirens. The Sirens were sisters who lived on a dangerous rock in the ocean. They sang so sweetly that the passing mariners forgot everything but their music and thus were often lured to shipwreck. Ulysses wanted to hear that enchanting music, but he did not want to die. So he plugged his oarsmen's ears with wax. Leaving his own ears open, he had himself tied firmly to the mast, lest the tempting sounds lure him to the rock. Thus, he was able to get through the perilous journey alive; his deafened sailors could hear neither the music nor his commands to free him.

We cannot make ourselves entirely deaf to temptation, but we can fine tune our hearing so that the ears of the heart become more sensitive to the less blaring sounds around us. "There are some less obvious sounds we need to tune our ears to hear," wrote Paul Tillich. "The sighing of innumerable lonely people all around us and over the world fills the ears that are opened by love."

The Tempting Sounds I Hear

Prayer: O Lord, we have become accustomed to seeing what we want to see and hearing what we want to hear. Turn us from the glittering distractions of novelty and the tempting sounds we hear. "O let us hear you speaking in accents clear and still. O give us grace to follow, my Master and my Friend." Amen.

Turn My Dreams to Noble Action

She was full of good works and acts of charity.
Acts 9:36b

Like the arching of the heavens,
Lift my thoughts above.
Turn my dreams to noble action,
Ministries of love.

God, Who Touchest Earth with Beauty
Mary S. Edgar

Woodrow Wilson, the twenty-eighth president of the United States, was a believer in dreams. He wrote, "We grow by dreams. All great men and women are dreamers. They see things in the soft haze of a spring day or in the red fire of a long winter's evening. Some of us let these great dreams die, but others nourish and protect them, nurse them through bad days 'till they bring them to the sunshine and light which comes always to those who hope that their dreams will come true."

When I was a child, one of our family's traditions was

to see who could be the first to spot a star at evening time. That person would then get to make a wish after reciting:

Star light, star bright
First star I see tonight,
I wish I may
I wish I might,
I wish my dream
Would come true tonight.

The wish was to be more than a passing fancy. It was to be something that was realistic and possible to achieve if we were willing to work toward making it happen. The hardest rule to follow was keeping the wish a secret. It could be shared only when it came true or was deemed unfulfillable. Although I didn't realize it at the time, I'm sure our parents wanted us to learn early in life that what we wished for we also had to work for.

All of us are dreamers! What we have dreamed or wished for may have changed according to the circumstances in our lives, but we continue to dream. Our dreams, hopes, aims will mark time, however, until we start them marching. They become true only when we act to turn them into realities.

When our daughter was very young, we traveled with some friends to visit their relatives in the western part of Virginia. Gail was intrigued with the change from the very flat area where we lived to the hills and then the mountains. As we proceeded around a curve, the mountains formed a beautiful panorama for us. She asked several times, "Who made the mountains?" The adults were busy with their own conversations and all but ignored her question. Finally, in exasperation she said, "I know if you don't. Someone planted hill seeds, and God make them grow." God had indeed provided not only the seeds but also the other raw materials that make the beautiful landscape for us to enjoy.

Yes, all of us are dreamers. Some of our dreams are very real and personal, and others are more altruistic. We may dream of owning a house with a beautiful garden or living in a better community in which to raise our children. We may dream of an end to hunger and poverty and a world free of hatred and war. But whatever dreams we may have can and will come true only if and when we are willing to act upon them.

Prayer: Gracious Lord, creator and sustainer of all life, forgive us when we fail to turn our dreams into ministries of love. Amen.

I Give Thee Back the Life I Owe

Hence I remind you to rekindle the gift of God that is within you . . .

2 Timothy 1:6

O Love that wilt not let me go,
I rest my weary soul in thee;
I give thee back the life I owe,
that in thine ocean depths
its flow may richer, fuller be.

O Love That Wilt Not Let Me Go
George Matheson

A part of being human seems to be to shortchange ourselves in comparison to others. This is especially true when focusing on our gifts or talents. We have often heard someone say, "I'd give my right arm if I could sing like Arlene, or play the piano like Ann, or pray like Henry. Oh, I can wash dishes and help clean. I give my used clothing and furniture to help the needy, but I really have so little talent to give."

The truth of the matter is that we all have gifts,

> *But each has his own special gift from God, one of one kind and one of another... Now there are varieties of gifts, but the same Spirit; and there are varieties of service, but the same Lord; and there are varieties of working, but it is the same God who inspires them all in every one.*
> I Corinthians 7:7b; 12:4–6

A young boy had a lunch of bread and fish. He gave what he had, and Jesus used it to feed a crowd of hungry people. Four men had the gifts of compassion and strength. They carried a paralytic to see Jesus, removed the roof, lifted him down on the pallet, and the man walked again. Some ordinary people in the little town of Bethsaida, near the Sea of Galilee, brought a blind man to Jesus and begged Jesus to touch him. And the man's sight was restored.

"We take different kinds of pleasure in giving," wrote Reverend David F. Lassalle in his newsletter while he was chaplain at Canterbury Center. "Perhaps the most exciting is the gift to a child so young he or she doesn't really know who the gift came from; the joy that the teddy bear or pull-toy produces is our reward, unmixed by an expectation of return . . . Perhaps the closest we can come to the pure gift is an anonymous one: a gift of volunteer work, of blood, or a contribution to charity. Such a gift, which can never be acknowledged or returned by those it comforts, can heal our spirits when they are wearied with too much ego."

A story I heard when I was very young continues to tug at my heart. The mother of three precious daughters was confined to a wheelchair. As her birthday approached, the two older girls began to do errands to earn some money to buy her a gift. The important day arrived and the oldest girl took three trays from the cabinet. One placed powder and a box of tissues on her tray. Another went to the kitchen and placed some new utensils on her tray. As the three entered their mother's room, the older girls noticed that their little sister's tray was empty. It was too late to share with her, but the little girl was not in the least perturbed. She simply placed her tray on the floor, stepped on it, and said, "Mother, I give you me."

Every living person has a precious gift to bestow on another. It is the gift of the heart.

Prayer: O Lord, help us to realize that we give but little when we give our possessions. Remind us that expressions of love are the best gifts of all. Amen.

Your Loving Kindnesses to Share

Let brotherly love continue. Do not neglect to show hospitality to strangers, for thereby some have entertained angels unawares.

Hebrews 13:1–2

Open my mouth, let me declare
Words of assurance everywhere;
Open my heart, and let me prepare
Your loving kindnesses to share.
Silently now I wait for You,
Ready, my God, Your will to do;
Open my heart, illumine me
Spirit divine.

Open My Eyes That I May See
Clara H. Scott

A church school teacher asked a young boy in her class to give a definition of loving-kindness. He replied, "Now, let me think a minute." Then he said, "If I was hungry and you gave me a piece of bread, that would be kindness. If you were to put jelly on the bread, that would be loving-kindness."

Kindness is the same in every language and every nation. It is recognizable wherever it is found. C. N. Bruce stated that "Kindness is a language the dumb can speak, and the deaf can hear and understand." It is positive action. It does something constructive.

Some years ago a story circulated regarding a famous Viennese surgeon who was visiting the United States. While he was here, many requests were made for his aid. The surgeon, who was an avid walker, set out one day in threatening weather. When a storm came up, a mother, who had wanted the doctor's help in curing her child, went out on the front porch to check the furniture. A gentleman walked toward the house and asked if he might sit out the storm on the porch. Indifferently, she agreed and went back into the house. A few minutes later someone came with a car and picked up the gentleman. The next day the local newspaper reported how the famous doctor had been marooned in a rainstorm and taken shelter on a porch. The woman, then recognizing who he was, rushed to the hotel where he was reported to be staying, only to learn he had just left. A missed opportunity to show kindness!

"I expect to pass through life but once. If there be any kindness I can show, or any good thing I can do to any fellow-being, let me do it now, and not defer or neglect it, as I should not pass this way again." These words, attributed to William Penn, the famous Quaker, speak to us as clearly today as they did when they were written some three hundred years ago.

We are inclined to think that everyone has life easier than we do. But never let us forget that each person we meet will be fighting some kind of personal battle. The kindness we show may be what he or she needs to help see it through.

Touched by a loving heart,
  Wakened by kindness,
Chords that are broken
  Will vibrate once more.

Fanny J. Crosby
Rescue the Perishing

Prayer: O Lord, we ask your blessings on all those everywhere in your world who plant kindness, not that they gather praise, but that they may bring hope and joy into otherwise drab lives. Teach us to use your gift of love that we may extend loving-kindness even on those days when we don't feel so kind. Amen.

Great Things He Hath Taught Us

" . . . Truly, I say to you, whoever does not receive the kingdom of God like a child shall not enter it."
Luke 18:17

Great things he hath taught us,
great things he hath done,
and great our rejoicing
thru Jesus the Son;
but purer, and higher,
and greater will be
our wonder, our transport,
when Jesus we see.

To God Be the Glory
Fanny J. Crosby

The word translated *teacher* is used forty-seven times in the New Testament to describe Jesus. Perhaps it was his favorite title. Even his enemies, like the Pharisees and the Herodians, recognized that one could learn from him. While he was preparing for entering the kingdom, some mothers brought their children to him for his blessing. In their pride and insensitivity, the disciples rebuked the children, but Jesus tells them that they must become as little children, or they will miss the kingdom of God altogether.

Nowhere in the Bible does Jesus ask children to become adults. But he did set a child in the midst of adults and told them to become like children. Why? "Being like a child to Jesus meant retaining the intuition of childhood," observed Frances Dunlap Heron in an article, "Faith to Work By." "It is the inner 'knowing' with which a child accepts each new miracle of the universe, the reverent trust in the unseen power back of the stars, the forgiving love, the ready laughter." Children are sensitive, humble, open, and filled with enthusiasm, adventure, and imagination.

A four-year-old girl was playing in the family's garden. After looking at the flowers for a while, she dropped on her knees beside a bed of jonquils and began to talk with great earnestness. An adult relative, noticing the child, stepped nearer and observed that the little girl had her lips close to the cup of a large jonquil as she talked. When she rose and left the flowers, the adult asked her why she was talking to the flower. The child, amazed at the ignorance of an adult, said, "I was telephoning to God. Didn't you know that those flowers are God's telephone?"

The design of the telephone as we know it today may not resemble that of the telephone used when Elizabeth McE Shields told this story, but the message is still the same—a child recognizes God in the beauty of a garden and pauses to say thanks.

Great Things He Hath Taught Us

There are no better examples of faith and forgiveness than those expressed by little children. Their faith is implicit and strong, and their trust in those they love is unwavering.

Perhaps we have become too sophisticated and skeptical to learn the lesson Jesus taught when he took a child and put him by his side. God is still full of surprises! We have not yet begun to see and enjoy all the miracles of his creation. But only those with the empty hands and joyous expectancy of children will receive the loving rule of God. He cannot give himself to us when our hands are tightly closed, protecting our own security, or when our hearts are overconfident in our own goodness and power.

Prayer: We confess, O Lord, that we have not begun to practice the great things you have taught us. Enable us by your spirit to come as little children with lives open to the freshness and surprises of each new day and the faith and trust to follow your teachings. Amen.

Speak Oft with Thy Lord

*Rejoice always, pray constantly, give thanks
in all circumstances . . .*
                  1 Thessalonians 5:16–18a

> Take time to be holy,
> speak oft with thy Lord;
> abide in him always,
> and feed on his word.
> Make friends of God's children;
> help those who are weak;
> forgetting in nothing
> God's blessing to seek.

Take Time to Be Holy
W. D. Longstaff

When I was younger, I loved the idea of playing the piano. I would picture myself giving a concert for all my family and friends in my hometown. Once the lessons had begun, the required daily practice soon took the edge off the fun and excitement. My mother would compliment me on how well I was doing, but then she would always add those words I didn't want to hear: "Don't forget, practice makes perfect." I learned to play well enough for my own enjoyment but never reached concert level because I liked to avoid those practice times.

Deepening our prayer life is an essential part of daily spiritual exercise, and it requires practice. Yet we are told that most Christians spend less than five minutes a day in prayer and even then we do all the talking. "One of the basic misconceptions about prayer," states L. Nelson Bell, "is that it is primarily asking God for things. The closer we live to God, the more prayer becomes a way of life, a realization of his nearness and availability at all times."

It was David's bedtime, and he was tired, so tired, from a hard day's play that his mother let him skip the usual preparations for bed. After only the very necessary things had been done, and as she tucked the weary little boy under the cover and kissed him goodnight, she said, "We'll have to skip prayers tonight because you are so tired." Then she turned out the light. Just as she was closing the door, a voice called, "Mommy-y-y, come back a minute, please." As she stood beside the bed, David said, "I can't skip prayers tonight. God gave me such a good day."

The discipline of prayer, like playing the piano, seems less important when the extracurricular activities of our lives crowd in upon us. It is then that we often lose sight of the source of our energy and strength. Our spiritual generating plant, as one person described it, is called *PRAYER,* and the only breakdown comes when we stop praying.

In one of his *Dennis the Menace* cartoons, Hank Ketcham shows Dennis and his friend walking home at dusk. The caption reads: "I say my prayers every night because God is a regular listener." Prayer is not something that can be occasionally indulged in. God *is* a regular listener, and we must follow Paul's injunction to pray without ceasing.

Prayer: Help us, O God, to cultivate an attitude of prayer for times of joy and for seasons of distress and grief. May we never become too busy or too tired to thank you for a good day. Amen.

Near the Cross I'll Watch and Wait

. . . If any man would come after me, let him deny himself and take up his cross and follow me . . . So, could you not watch with me one hour? . . .
Matthew 16:24; 26:40

Near the cross I'll watch and wait,
Hoping, trusting ever,
'Til I reach the golden strand
Just beyond the river.
In the cross, in the cross,
Be my glory ever,
'Til my raptured soul shall find
Rest beyond the river.

Near the Cross
Fanny J. Crosby

Every ten years thousands from around the world travel to Germany to witness the famous Passion Play at Oberammergau. The highlight of any visit is to meet personally with the actors, especially since they are all local residents. An American couple had the chance to visit with the actor who was playing the part of Christ just as he was preparing for the scene in which the Via Dolorosa to Calvary is portrayed. The woman suggested to her husband that perhaps she could take his picture with the cross. They politely asked the actor if they could use his cross for a moment. When he agreed to their request, the husband bent to lift the cross on his back, but it was too heavy. "Why do you make it so heavy?" he asked. "One made of papier-mâché would work just as well." The actor replied, "Sir, I could not play the part of Christ if I did not feel the weight of the cross."

An impatient teenager who was bothered because she had to wait in line so long for confession complained to the church administration. "You should be more efficient," she said. "You ought to have a fast line for those with three sins or less."

Both of these experiences remind us of the times in which we live. How quickly we become dependent on courtesy clerks who carry our packages and express lines that mean we seldom have to wait. Worship services are scheduled for our convenience, and "dial-a-prayer" is available around the clock.

Watching and waiting near the cross is not a preferred pastime in our lives. We opt for an easier life and try to avoid hardship and suffering at any cost. We recoil from pain instinctively; we shrink from conflict easily. When making decisions, we often choose the easiest way out.

No one of us is ever forced to be a Christian, but once we voluntarily declare ourselves as a disciple of Jesus, there are definite requirements. One is that we be willing to take up our cross, no matter how heavy, and follow him. This means deliberately taking upon ourselves a burden we are not compelled to take at all. It means deliberately choosing something that could be avoided, even taking upon ourselves the burden of others.

A church school teacher once concluded a lesson with these words: "Jesus felt the cross in his heart long before he felt it on his shoulders. Can we do otherwise?"

Prayer: Create in me a loving heart, O Lord, and place the right spirit within me that I may be willing to travel the uncomfortable roads and share the pain and heartaches of others. Amen.

Sometimes I Feel Discouraged

Cast all your anxieties on him, for he cares about you.
1 Peter 5:7

There is a balm in Gilead
to make the wounded whole,
there is a balm in Gilead
to heal the sin-sick soul.
Sometimes I feel discouraged
and think my work's in vain,
but then the Holy Spirit
revives my soul again.

There Is a Balm in Gilead
African-American Spiritual

"Life is like an ice cream cone," commented a friend. Just when you think you've got it licked, it drips on you." It is doubtful whether anyone's life will go exactly as planned, or if it will turn out the way one would wish. There certainly will be times when we feel dripped upon. We will pass through periods of comfort and joy and then periods of distress. There will be days when we will not feel like singing, when the sun is hidden behind the clouds. Sometimes we may be tormented by financial problems, family responsibilities, poor health, or other burdens. At times, we will feel as if we have reached the place that some call *wits end* or what others may call *the end of the rope.*

The words of Emerson are helpful when facing these discouraging times. He wrote:

> *Don't waste time in doubts and fears; spend yourself in the work before you, well assured that the right performance of this hour's duties will be the best preparation for the hours or ages that follow.*

God did not design us for weakness, sickness, frustration, or failure. God planted within us wonderful potentialities of health, strength, happiness, progress, and success. How we learn to cope with the problems of life, how we respond to our hardships and discouraging times, and what we learn in overcoming them—that's what will strengthen us from within and allow us to regain our courage and renew our faith.

A teacher asked a class of children, "How many can name the four chief points on the compass?" One boy said, "But there are five points." The teacher replied, "I thought there were four. You name the five." The boy responded, "North, east, south, and west, and the place right where you are."

God meets us and helps us to take control of our lives again, right where we are. He may not change the circumstances for us, but he will always offer grace to overcome them. We will find him waiting to comfort, to heal, to inspire, and to give us the promise of renewed joy.

> *Got any rivers you think are uncrossable?*
> *Got any mountains you can't tunnel*
>   *through?*
> *God specializes in things thought impossible.*
> *He can do what others cannot do.*
>   Author Unknown

Prayer: Strengthen us, O Lord, whenever we are disappointed or become discouraged. Give us faith that will enable us to grow stronger in all circumstances. Help us to learn to rely more on you. When we fail, give us the courage to try again. Amen.

Change and Decay in All Around I See

For I the Lord do not change . . .
Malachi 3:6

Swift to its close
ebbs out life's little day;
earth's joys grow dim;
its glories pass away;
change and decay in all around I see;
O thou who changest not,
abide with me.

Abide with Me
Henry F. Lyte

Three thousand years ago a Greek professor named Heraclitus taught his students that all of reality is in constant flux. Nothing is stable. Life, he said, was like a river. You could never step twice into the same river because during the time you stepped out, the flowing water your feet had first touched would have passed by.

In many ways the insight of that ancient philosopher describes well our present situation of rapid change. Not only does everything seem to be changing, but also the speed of change is accelerating. As Gabriel noted from his heavenly perch in Marc Connelly's play *Green Pastures*, "Everything nailed down is coming loose."

Change at a rapid pace can be quite unsettling. Yet we can find balance when we acknowledge that since the beginning of history God's people have had to find new ways of thinking and living to meet ever-changing conditions of their times.

Jefferson T. Kesterson, a Presbyterian minister, refers to God as the great changer in history. He observes that he is still busy turning things around, turning things upside down, tearing down dividing walls, and making things over. One might conclude that God planned the universe so that things are constantly changing. In some places the seasons change from hour to hour. Today has never been a complete repeat of yesterday. People never stand still either. Our experiences make us changing people.

When Dr. Henry Francis Lyte, a native of Ednam, Scotland, wrote the words of the hymn "Abide with Me," he was an old man, near the end of his life's journey. He was tired and in poor health. His doctor, who had given him only a few months to live, suggested that he move to a warmer climate. One account relates that while he was sitting at his desk thinking about his doctor's suggestion, he picked up his Bible to read. It fell open to one of his favorite passages in Luke. He read: *"Abide with us: for it is toward evening, and the day is far spent . . ."* (Luke 24:29 KJV)

Change and Decay in All Around I See

After reading and re-reading those words, he felt refreshed and began writing:

> *Abide with me; fast falls the eventide;*
> *the darkness deepens, God with me abide . . .*
> *change and decay in all around I see;*
> *O thou who changest not, abide with me.*

Change and what we may perceive as decay are the only things that seem certain these days. But we need to remember that the love of God will never change. He alone is the rock. We can count on that!

Prayer: Thank you, O Lord, for your constant presence in our lives and for the assurance that amid all the changes in life we can count on you to be there for us. Amen.

Be Thou My Guide

He will be our guide for ever.
Psalm 48:14

While life's dark maze I tread,
and griefs around me spread,
be thou my guide;
bid darkness turn to day;
wipe sorrow's tears away;
nor let me ever stray
from thee aside.

My Faith Looks Up to Thee
Ray Palmer

The conference grounds were bubbling with excitement as a hundred or so teenagers dispersed in all directions to take advantage of scheduled free time. Later, as I sat on the porch enjoying my rocking chair, two conferees, obviously out of breath, dropped down on the steps in front of me. When I asked them what they had been doing, one replied: "Oh, we were hiking to the water tower, but we climbed the wrong mountain."

Be Thou My Guide

Many of us have had the same experience. We have been so engrossed in climbing the mountain that we paid little or no attention to the direction we were going. Laboring under the false impression that the important thing was to be climbing, no matter where, we gained little but exhaustion.

There just seems to be something about us humans that makes us resist following directions or admitting we need help in solving a problem. Think of the hours we have spent trying to get some newly purchased gadget to operate properly. Or consider the energy we spent assembling a child's toy at Christmas only to find the train still jumped the track after we had put it together just the way we concluded it should be. That's when someone close by reminds us, "When all else fails, it helps to read the directions."

A few of us might feel a kinship with the businessman who chartered a small airplane to save time and to squeeze more into a day. After a while, he leaned forward to the pilot and asked, "How are we doing?" The pilot is said to have replied, "We're making good time, but we're lost."

Some things about God seem so big and wonderful that we cannot imagine his being with us everywhere. But we must know that it is true. He is never far away and is always there ready, to be our guide forever. The problem is not with him but with us. We want to do things our way until we get lost, or our lives begin to take a wrong turn. It is then that we ask him for directions. If we put our ultimate hope in ourselves and our own know-how, we are asking in advance to be disappointed. But if we learn to place our trust in him and seek his guiding hand, we will find the strength and the guidance that we need to proceed on our journey.

Prayer: O God, you are able to still all kinds of storms and to give calm as well as guidance to those who ask. Help us to remember to ask you for help and thank you for being willing to give it. Enable us to open the windows of our minds and hearts to your presence in order that we may yield ourselves to your guidance. Amen.

Teach Me the Patience of Unanswered Prayer

But if we hope for what we do not see, we wait for it with patience.

Romans 8:25

Teach me to feel
that thou art always nigh;
teach me the struggles of the soul to bear:
to check the rising doubt,
the rebel sigh;
teach me the patience of unanswered prayer.

Spirit of God, Descend upon My Heart
George Croly

The code words for today seem to be *instant* and *fast*. We can satisfy our cravings for food in a fast food restaurant or with an instant breakfast, a cup of instant coffee or tea, or with instant soup. Then we can hurry off to get an instant passport picture, some instant printing completed, and run our car through the quickie car wash. We can purchase updated computers, fax machines, and household gadgets that promise to save us even more time than the previous models.

Living in this age of *instants* makes patience more difficult, especially if we try to transfer this fast pace into other areas of our lives. We could come to expect immediate solutions to difficult problems over which we have prayed and conclude, if there is a delay, that our prayers have gone unanswered. But God is always right on time. He continually weaves the answers to our requests so cleverly into the patterns of our life that we are tempted to doubt whether he has acted at all. Our prayers may have been answered but not exactly as we prayed them.

In Lloyd C. Douglas' *The Big Fisherman*, a Roman officer prays for Peter's life. Peter is condemned to die. The officer says, "I have prayed for you but it hasn't done any good." "I'm sure it has," says Peter, "I haven't been afraid."

"Some people tend to think of prayer as a rope attaching a huge ship to a little boat," writes Jill Briscoe in the book *Hush! Hush!* "They are the boat and the big ship is God's will. They think the rope of prayer is to be used to pull the big ship alongside their little boat. This is against all natural laws, just as it is against all spiritual laws to say, 'Not Thy will, but mine be done!' Obviously, what has to happen as we pull on the rope of obedience in prayer is that the little boat draws alongside of the big ship and sails wherever the big ship wills."

A friend recently related an experience she and her husband had on a tour of the Holy Land. The group had visited St. Catherine's Monastery at the foot of Mt. Sinai. Some of the group decided to climb the mountain. The temperature had reached over 104 degrees as they began their descent. While some of them were able to make it down without too much difficulty, word came that several others were having problems. As this news was received, some of the group gathered in a circle and began to pray for the safety of their fellow travelers. In the meantime, my friend's husband, although he was very tired, had already gone back up the mountain to help the others down.

Some of our prayers will never make it if we just pour out petitions without taking the time to see if there is something we can do to bring about an answer. Dwight L. Moody once said, "There is no use asking God to do things you can do for yourself."

Prayer: Give us patience to wait for your answer, O God, as we pray "not my will but thine be done." Amen.

Look Up and Laugh and Love and Lift

Then our mouth was filled with laughter, and our
tongue with shouts of joy . . .
Psalm 126:2

I would be friend of all—the foe, the friendless;
    I would be giving, and forget the gift;
I would be humble, for I know my weakness;
    I would look up, and laugh, and love, and lift,
I would look up, and laugh, and love, and lift.

I Would Be True
Howard Arnold Walter

"Laughter has proven to be the lubricant of life any occasions," wrote Roy L. Smith in an issue of the *Upper Room*, a bi-monthly devotional. "We can laugh our way over many a difficulty we cannot climb over, and we can smile our way through situations we cannot get through in any other way."

Personal experience will attest to the truth of this. Several years ago I was in the hospital being prepared late one night to undergo bypass surgery the next morning. Everything was progressing normally when suddenly the whole hospital became darkened. We learned later that a backhoe operator at the construction site behind the hospital had cut a cable. Emergency generators restored electricity to critical areas, but only a minimum of light was available in the rooms and hallways. My nurse, Flo, who had left the room to get a flashlight, returned to tell me that we'd have to finish my prepping in the utility closet where there was water and some light. The next few minutes were filled with unexpected laughter as we tried to make the best of a difficult situation. We both became soaked as my scrub-down and iodine preparation were completed from a utility tub. We still laugh about it, and she declares that no nurse and patient have ever laughed so much together prior to surgery. Sometimes laughter can be therapeutic—the best medicine.

To permit oneself to laugh when the skies are dark and gray and to look up and sing when there is no other music to be heard may be difficult, but it is never impossible.

The preacher in the Book of Ecclesiastes reminds us that

> *For everything there is a season and a time for every matter under heaven*
>
> . . . .
>
> *a time to weep, and a time to laugh;*
> *a time to mourn, and a time to dance . . .*
>
> Ecclesiastes 3:1, 4

There is even a time to laugh at oneself. We need to learn not to take the sharp turns and mistakes we make in

127

life too seriously. As Seneca, the famous Roman stoic philosopher and author, wrote, "Whenever I wish to enjoy the quips of a clown, I am not compelled to look far; I can laugh at myself."

> *Go build of your worries a strong box,*
> *Have every part strengthened with care,*
> *When as strong as your efforts can make it*
> *Corral all your thoughts right there.*
> *Store in it all thoughts of failure*
> *And each bitter cup that you drink,*
> *Lock all your heartaches within it,*
> *Then—*
>
> > *sit on the lid—*
> > *and LAUGH.*
> > Author Unknown

What we need more than anything as we try to cope in today's world are laughing hearts that enable us to look up, laugh, love, and lift. God will be right there with us on our journey.

Prayer: Open up our hearts, compassionate Lord, and let the sunshine in. Help us to laugh when we feel more like crying; to sing for joy when all the things that make us joyful seem to have eluded us. Turn our heartaches into prayers of gratitude. Amen.

O, Tread the City's Streets Again

*But seek the welfare of the city where I have sent you
into exile, and pray to the LORD on its behalf, for in
its welfare you will find your welfare.*
Jeremiah 29:7

O Savior, from the mountainside,
make haste to heal these hearts of pain;
among these restless throngs abide;
O, tread the city's streets again.

Where Cross the Crowded Ways of Life
Frank Mason North

Wherever we look today, we experience brokenness, pain, and hurt. The human condition is tragic and critical. Walk the streets of our cities and towns and see that modern life is filled with puzzling contradictions. There we find the homeless, the unemployed and underemployed, the sick, the alcoholic, the drug abuser, and the lonely seeking companionship.

There we also find those who rely on the city for their livelihood: merchants, sales associates, restaurant owners, government officials, social workers and health providers.

As we walk through the city, we see it from many points of view. If we work for the bureau of tourism, we will see it differently than if we work for the health or welfare department. If we own a business or are landlords, we will see it differently than the homeless and those who must rely on public assistance simply to survive.

Undoubtedly, similar differences existed in Jesus' time. The scribes and the Pharisees probably saw Jerusalem differently than those who needed help. Perhaps very few persons actually saw it as Jesus saw it. Luke tells us, *"And when he drew near and saw the city* (Jerusalem) *he wept over it."* (Luke 19:41)

As we tread the cities' streets on his behalf, we do see evidence that someone cares. We find shelters, feeding programs, day care centers, employment and rehabilitation services, and programs like CARITAS.

CARITAS (Congregations Around Richmond Involved to Assure Shelter) is a coalition of some eighty church congregations that came together to help the homeless through the winter. Each night four congregations open their church doors as a place for the homeless to stay. Volunteers prepare and serve meals, provide clothing, health supplies, and recreational activities, and visit with the guests.

One evening the need for men's shoes was very evident. Although there were shoes available, none were the size one gentleman needed. When one of the volunteers looked at the man's feet and realized that his own shoes were the size needed, he removed his shoes and placed them on his new friend's feet. Later, when he was asked why he would do such a thing, he replied, "Remember, I still have socks."

First we must hear the call; next we must obey it.

Prayer: O God of the city, help us to go where the people are and minister in your name. Amen.

Drop Thy Still Dews of Quietness

*Then they cried to the L*ORD *in their trouble,*
and he delivered them from their distress;
he made the storm be still,
and the waves of the sea were hushed.
Then they were glad because they had quiet, and he
brought them to their desired haven.
Psalm 107:28–30

Drop thy still dews of quietness,
till all our strivings cease;
take from our souls the strain and stress,
and let our ordered lives confess
the beauty of thy peace.

Dear Lord, and Father of Mankind
John Greenleaf Whittier

How often have we heard a mother tell or even scream at a child to be quiet or a teacher tell the class to BE QUIET NOW! "Be quiet," they say. What is it they want the child or the class to do? Do they want them to cease talking, stop making noise, put their brains and thinking on hold, or do they want them to give them their attention and listen to what they have to say?

What is quietness? Is it the absence of noise, or is it a state of mind? Is it the absence of interruptions and distractions or the absence of fear and stress? Is it stillness with no activity, or is it a stillness that permits the mind and soul to be uncluttered and free?

Dietrich Bonhoeffer, the German theologian, wrote, "Anyone who thinks that his time is too valuable to spend keeping quiet will eventually have no time for God and his brother, but only for himself and for his follies." Have we reached the point in our lives where setting aside a time for keeping quiet has become a burden rather than a joy?

Henri J. M. Nouwen stated, "We have become so used to this state of anesthesia that we panic when there is nothing or nobody left to distract us. When we have no project to finish, no friend to visit, no book to read, no television to watch, and when we are left all alone by ourselves, we are brought so close to the revelation of our basic human aloneness . . . that we will do anything to get busy again."

Does God ever tell us to be quiet? Through the psalmist we are instructed to

> "Be still, and know that I am God . . .
> Be still before the LORD, and wait patiently for him;
> fret not yourself over him who prospers in his
> way . . ." (Psalm 46:10; 37:7)

Isaiah gets our attention with

For thus said the Lord God, the Holy One of Israel, "In returning and rest you shall be saved; in quietness and in trust shall be your strength." (Isaiah 30:15)

It is in quietness that we find God's presence which can bring growth and hope into our lives. It is in the stillness and calm that God comes to us and guides us as we chart the course of our daily lives.

Drop thy still dews of quietness

. . . .

Speak through the earthquake, wind and fire,
O still small voice of calm!

Prayer: Our Father, help us to treat our quiet moments with reverence. Help us to listen to you in the quiet today. May we be prepared for the surprises you permit us to hear. Amen.

Cure Thy Children's Warring Madness

Let us then pursue what makes for peace and for mutual upbuilding.

Romans 14:19

Cure thy children's warring madness;
bend our pride to thy control;
Shame our wanton, selfish gladness,
Rich in things and poor in soul.
Grant us wisdom, grant us courage,
lest we miss thy righteous goal,
lest we miss thy righteous goal.

God of Grace and God of Glory
Harry Emerson Fosdick

To be peacemakers in a world of violence and hatred is not easy, nor can we easily avoid the feeling of anger when there is so much oppression depicted before us. It is often difficult to avoid covetousness in a world saturated with material things. Sometimes we cannot even live at peace with those with whom we work or with those who live in the same house with us. We become easily irritated for little or no reason. It may be a small thing but it becomes like a grit or a small stone in our shoe. It then causes us to be uncomfortable all day.

A friend, finding herself needing to assist an aging parent with shopping and medical visits, commented that it wasn't the extra responsibility and time that irritated her; it was the parent's seemingly ungrateful attitude. An early morning trip to the grocery store sometimes left her with an angry feeling that she found hard to overcome.

If we have a tough time getting along with those close at hand, how much more difficult it is to live peaceably with our neighbors far away. We know so little about God's children, our brothers and sisters, in other parts of the world. Many of us have never touched a skin of a color other than our own. And so we let color or language or custom become barriers or even war zones in our minds, thus making peaceful relationships impossible.

No one of us can bring all the nations to a regard for Jesus Christ. But we can each become responsible, with God's help, for reaching out to one another and curing the warring madness which exists in that part of the world that is right around us.

In his book *Deep Is the Hunger,* Howard Thurman states, "It is so easy to underrate the potential power of one word spoken at the critical moment. We say to ourselves sometimes that, because we are not famous or learned or rich or powerful, or gifted, our word means nothing in the presence of a great injustice. Who would pay attention to us?" He reminds us that, "During practically any week we may be faced with some great wrong, or some simple but gross expression of injustice and there is no one to speak but you. Do not be silent. There is no limit to the power that may be released through us."

God wants us to live holy and peaceful lives. It may seem strange that holiness and peaceable living are seen as parts of the same fabric. But right relationships with God cannot be separated from right relationships with the persons around us.

> *Walk together, talk together*
> *O ye people of the earth;*
> *Then and only then shall you have peace.*
> Sanskrit

Prayer: We wait now in your presence, O Lord, for something to transpire within us that will relax the hold we have on the things that do not make for peace. Cure your children's warring madness here at home and throughout the world. Bind our pride to your control. Amen.

Whispers of Love

And above all these put on love, which binds every
thing together in perfect harmony.
                                Colossians 3:14

Perfect submission, perfect delight,
visions of rapture now burst on my sight;
angels descending bring from above
echoes of mercy, whispers of love.
This is my story, this is my song,
praising my Savior all the day long;
this is my story, this is my song,
praising my Savior all the day long.

Blessed Assurance
Fanny J. Crosby

Several years ago I was serving as supply pastor for
a small congregation some seventy-five miles from
my home. This particular morning I was traveling
down the interstate highway when I began thinking almost
out loud, to myself: *Why am I doing this? I have worked*
hard all week and feel so tired and weary. I have so little time

and energy to give these folks. What can I possibly do for them that someone else couldn't do better?

When I parked in front of the church a few minutes later, the usual greeters were there to welcome me and say how happy they were that I had taken the time to come.

At eleven o'clock the service began, and the small group of God's faithful joined in singing:

angels descending bring from above
echoes of mercy, whispers of love.

This fascinating combination of words penned by Fanny J. Crosby in the hymn "Blessed Assurance" leaped out at me as they had never done before. I almost lost my place as I thought to myself: *That's it! That's what I can give, whispers of love. I don't have to perform great miracles or feel that I have to assist them in becoming what they aren't or can never be. All I am called to do is share with them and help them to share whispers of love with others.*

Love is the most universally desired quality in the world—the high and the low, the rich and the poor, the young and the old—all crave acts of love. It is also the most enduring thing in the world. Under pressure, tension, or suffering, it shines most brightly. It never fails. It endures.

But whoever saw love? It is like the wind. It is felt. Its presence is recognized through things that are seen. It is a happening. It can become known through a friendly hand-shake, a warm embrace, or some deed of kindness.

Jesus gave repeated and surprising emphasis to what many have called obscure service—service with little or no fanfare. He spoke of the importance of the cup of cold water given in love. He insisted that to feed the hungry and visit the sick was of infinite value.

We come in daily contact with persons who need our love, but we fail to act because we feel that what we have to offer is so small or insignifcant compared to what someone else might provide. Let us not forget that a friendly word— a whisper of love—could cleanse the heart, banish doubt, or conquer fear.

Prayer: O Lord, teach us the worth of a small deed, and remind us how many there are who need a smile or a friendly hand. Help us to remember that often people need our love most when they are unlovable and filled with bitterness and anger. Use us as channels of your blessings through our whispers of love. Amen.

With Heart and Hands and Voices

You will seek me and find me; when you seek me with all your heart, I will be found by you, says the LORD.

Jeremiah 29:13–14a

Now thank we all our God
with heart and hands and voices,
who wondrous things has done,
in whom the world rejoices,
who, from our mothers' arms,
has blessed us on our way
with countless gifts of love,
and still is ours today.

Now Thank We All Our God
Martin Rinkart

From the 1600s comes a story of a little boy named Antonio who was sharing a holiday with his two special friends in the crowded streets of their hometown in Italy. On such special festival days boys sang and played for the happy crowds who expressed their appreciation by giving them coins.

Salvatore and Gulio stood making plans. Salvatore was to sing, and Gulio was to play the violin. They invited little Antonio to come along even though they knew he couldn't sing or play. All he could do was whittle.

Many folks came by, listened, and shared coins with them. The boys were not too surprised when one man gave them a gold piece, for they knew he could afford it. The man was Nicolo Amati, the famous master of violin making. Several days after the festival, Antonio went to visit Mr. Amati and showed him his carvings, hoping he would teach him to carve violins. "Why do you want to make violins?" asked Mr. Amati, "It is good to make violins, but the song in the heart is what matters." Antonio Stradivari, who became Mr. Amati's greatest pupil, is still regarded as the greatest violin maker of all time.

The song in the heart is what matters! It can bring an upsurge of joy in living that will give us strength to use our hands and voices in expressing our thanksgiving through acts of love and concern.

There are many ways of expressing the song in the heart. Some can sing, some can paint, some can grow flowers. Others can visit the sick and shut-ins, while others make telephone calls. Many can offer prayers of praise, healing, and thanksgiving in the good times and in the turbulent times.

There is a true story about the Reverend Martin Rinkart, who gave thanks even though he had great difficulty in finding enough food and clothing for his children. His country had just been through a war that had lasted thirty years. In the midst of all these calamities, Rinkart and many people of his country remained faithful to their religious beliefs and kept a song in their hearts. So true was his faith and love for God that he wrote the well-known hymn "Now Thank We All Our God." The hymn was written in German as a song of praise because peace had come to his country.

> *O may this bounteous God*
> *through all our life be near us,*
> *with ever joyful hearts*
> *and blessed peace to cheer us . . .*

Prayer: Thank you, O Lord for placing a song in our hearts. Strengthen and guide us as we live from day to day that we may sing praises and share your love, no matter what the circumstances. Amen.

Tune My Heart to Sing Thy Grace

But the LORD *said to Samuel, "Do not look on his appearance or on the height of his stature, because I have rejected him; for the* LORD *sees not as man sees; man looks on the outward appearance, but the* LORD *looks on the heart."*
1 Samuel 16:7

Come, thou Fount of every blessing,
tune my heart to sing thy grace;
streams of mercy, never ceasing,
call for songs of loudest praise.
Teach me some melodious sonnet,
sung by flaming tongues above.
Praise the mount! I'm fixed upon it,
mount of thy redeeming love.

Come, Thou Fount of Every Blessing
Robert Robinson

One day, after months of neglecting to play the piano, I found that it was terribly out of tune. The local music store came to my rescue and sent a piano tuner to correct the problem. The tuner used a tuning fork, a simple tone-producing U-shaped object, to find the standard pitch as he carefully struck each note. He told me that the tuning fork would always remain the same because it was not subject to the changes resulting from temperature and moisture that may affect the pitch and tone of musical instruments. After an hour or two of carefully striking, listening, adjusting, the piano was like new again.

Human lives sometimes become out of tune like a musical instrument. The Jews, amid all the grandeur of the temple, loved to sing the songs of Zion. But when taken captive to far-off Babylon, they asked, "How shall we sing the Lord's song in a strange land?"

There are times in the experience of all of us when the desire to sing seems to have gone out of our hearts. When this happens, Jesus Christ is our tuning fork. From him, we can find the standard for our lives. He is always there to listen, fine tune, and help to make the needed adjustments.

Sometimes, however, we try to correct the sour notes by attending to the outward appearance. We try to keep smiles on our faces and volunteer to do the right things in our churches and communities. We do whatever is necessary to stay busy. But all of these fail to make us happy because our hearts are still out of tune. Our intentions may be good and noble, but we may be doing the right things for the wrong reason. Perhaps our actions are self-fulfilling rather than geared toward meeting the real needs of those we seek to help.

In *Prayer in the Contemporary World*, Douglas V. Steere relates an interesting experience of Dr. Albert Schweitzer's. One day Dr. Schweitzer made a safari into the jungle regions of Africa to get to know the area from which most of his hospital patients came. The word of his coming went before him by the drums—the jungle telegraph—telling people what path he was taking and where they might bring their sick to see him. At one crossway, Dr. Schweitzer met a beautiful girl whom the group asked him to treat. Outwardly, she seemed in perfect health. But when he asked what was wrong with her, they replied in their own way that she speaks with her eyes, and she hears with her heart—for she was deaf and dumb. "The world is suffering today from too few people who hear with their hearts," concludes Mr. Steere.

Prayer: O heavenly Father, draw close and give us hearing hearts. Unfold your love and inner beauty that our hearts may be tuned to go forth and sing your grace all the day long. Amen.

Rejoice, Give Thanks and Sing

Rejoice always, pray constantly, give thanks in all circumstances; for this is the will of God in Christ Jesus for you.

1 Thessalonians 5:16

Rejoice, you pure in heart;
lift praises to the sky;
your festive banner wave with joy,
the cross of Christ raise high!
Rejoice, rejoice,
rejoice, give thanks and sing.

Rejoice, You Pure in Heart
Edward H. Plumptre

My first grandson was placed in the pediatric intensive care unit shortly after his birth. His mother began her visits to the unit to feed him as soon as the physicians would allow. When she was discharged, Jason remained hospitalized, but she returned to the hospital several times a day to feed him and to be with him. One day when she came into the waiting room where I had been sitting, she said, "I think he likes 'Winnie the Pooh' the best." I learned then that she had been not only feeding him but also rocking and singing to him almost since his birth. Even under extremely difficult circumstances and with much anguish in her heart, she was able to rejoice, give thanks and sing.

Rejoice, what a verb that is!

The shepherd rejoices more over the one than over the ninety-nine that never were lost. The father rejoices over the return of his son who was lost and is found. Strange? Not really. They did not love the others less, but now thankfulness has been added.

We do not need to wait for a special day or time of the year to offer thanks. The thankful spirit is like the loving heart; it is ours because of the way we feel and respond to life. No one can command us to have a thankful spirit. This is the inner realm where we have dominion.

No one person has more capacity for thankfulness than another. The thankful spirit is in all of us. Someone has said that "the very nature of our being is to be thankful. If we could hear them, it is likely that the very cells of our body sing for joy." When we do not feel thankful, we do not really feel alive. We feel something is missing, for thankfulness is an attitude. If we wait until our family is in perfect health and we have no sorrow, no trouble, and no anxieties, we will never give thanks.

The Bible is filled with thanksgiving on the part of people fully aware of the perils of their time. Daniel, when threatened with death, " . . . *went to his house where he had windows in his upper chamber open toward Jerusalem; and he got down upon his knees three times a day and prayed and gave thanks before his God, as he had done previously."* (Daniel 6:10) Paul and Silas sang praises to God while in prison. Jesus, on the night when he was betrayed, took bread and broke it and gave thanks. During the good times and the bad, each of us must move forth in faith with an ongoing song in our heart.

Prayer: Dear Lord, help us to learn that even in the dark times of our lives, we can find reason to give you thanks for being with us each step of the way. Amen.

The Sympathizing Tear

To make an apt answer is a joy to a man,
and a word in season, how good it is!
Proverbs 15:23

We share each other's woes,
Each other's burdens bear,
And often for each other flows
The sympathizing tear.

Blest Be the Tie That Binds
John Fawcett

S cience defines a tear as a drop of saline liquid secreted by the lacrimal gland. Tears bathe the eye and help clear it of foreign particles such as dust and hairs and keep it from drying out, which could result in blindness. Larry K. Waltz relates that "science can tell us what a tear is but God can assist us in the why."

When do tears come to our eyes? Do our eyes become moistened when we view a sad movie, a hurricane or other disaster on television, listen to a presentation on famine or homelessness, or hear of the loss of a friend or loved one?

"There's a lot of sympathy in the world," said a friend talking about a worthy project for which she was soliciting funds. "Most people are willing to give to charity." What she said was true, but sympathy is not always enough. Sympathy is feeling *for* someone; it is an easy sentiment, especially when we ourselves are unthreatened. We also need empathy, the feeling *with* someone, the projecting of our consciousness into his or her suffering.

Prior to open heart surgery, I heard from individuals who had been through a similar experience or had relatives who had kept telling me that I would shed a lot of tears the first few months afterwards. They were right! For seemingly no reason at all I would burst into tears. Following a good cry, I felt better even though I could not explain why I was crying. These weren't sympathizing tears, but they did bring release of feelings. Since that experience I have been better able to empathize with others facing the same or similar situation. I have been able to shed tears with them and assure them that times would get better.

Sometimes it is in our own suffering, failures, and disappointments that we learn to be empathetic with the suffering and heartaches of others. When a person is confronted with personal or family problems or the death of a friend or family member, our understanding and concern may not be able to eradicate all of the hurts, but our caring will help ease the pain and make the difficulty more bearable.

Plato, the Greek philosopher, once pointed out that we do not say, "My finger has a pain." We say, "I have a pain." When someone else hurts, we have a pain also. We shed a sympathizing tear. Even amid terrible suffering, Christ could be kind to a fellow sufferer. Thus, he set for us an unforgettable example of unselfish thinking and compassion for others.

> *. . . if a man is overtaken in any trespass, you who are spiritual should restore him in a spirit of gentle ness . . . Bear one another's burdens . . . as we have opportunity, let us do good to all . . .*
> Galatians 6:1, 2, 10.

Prayer: O Lord, make us this day a channel through which your love and your grace may flow. Amen.

Hold Me with Thy Powerful Hand

In his hand are the depths of the earth;
the heights of the mountains are his also.
The sea is his, for he made it;
for his hands formed the dry land.

Psalm 95:4–5

Guide me, O thou great Jehovah,
pilgrim through this barren land;
I am weak, but thou art mighty;
hold me with thy powerful hand;
bread of heaven, bread of heaven,
   feed me till I want no more,
   feed me till I want no more.

Guide Me, O Thou Great Jehovah
William Williams

We live in a world filled with unrest, fired by social injustice, political corruption, and economic upheaval. We experience times that are paralyzing us, causing us to be fearful of travel, mistrustful of individuals and nations, and limiting our mobility both within and outside our nation. These conditions, coupled with the increase in drug and alcohol addiction, could cause us to throw up our hands in despair and cry out, "Enough is enough, Lord. We thought you cared about your world. Why is this happening to us?"

"The world is not a marble which has slipped out of God's pocket, but a round globe which he loves," writes Halford E. Luccock in his book *Communicating the Gospel*. John in his Gospel describes for us a comforting picture. *". . . and no one is able to snatch them out of the Father's hand."* (John 10:29). We need to remind ourselves that we are in God's hands, and there we can remain secure. No matter what the circumstances, God will never leave us.

In his book *But God Can*, Robert V. Ozment tells the story about a father and his son who went mountain climbing. There were steep and dangerous places on the path they chose. As they were climbing one of those treacherous places, someone called out to the boy, "Do you have a good hold on your father, lad?" The boy replied, "No, but he has a good hold on me." God has a firm grip on the world as he holds it lovingly in his hands. One needs only to walk through refugee camps and talk with the displaced persons and those who voluntarily care for them to know that he cares for all who reside there.

God continues actively to hold the world through all the scientific and technological advances. He reaches down to his creation, whether as human beings they reside in refugee camps, the inner city, the suburbs, or the remote areas of the earth.

Hold Me With Thy Powerful Hand

We can all witness the spirit of God at work in the world, renewing society from within and transforming the relationships of people and nations. God cannot and will not forsake us, for we are all graven in the palms of his hands. The woman taken in adultery fell at Jesus' feet, and he heard the accusation of the mob. He saw hate ready to throw the stones that would take her life. With a loving hand, he reached down to lift her up and said, *"Neither do I condemn you; go, and sin no more."* (John 8:11) *"In his hand is the life of everything and the breath of all mankind."* (Job 12:10) As we extend our outstretched hands to others, we become partners with him in healing the brokenness that exists in the world, beginning right where we live.

Prayer: Thank you Lord, for holding each one of us as individuals, as families, as churches, and as nations in your powerful hand. Tighten your grip on us when we begin to slip away from your presence. Amen.

Wing Your Flight O'er All the Earth

. . ."you shall be my witnesses . . .
Acts 1:8

. . . thanks be to God, who in Christ always leads us
in triumph, and through us spreads the fragrance of
the knowledge of him everywhere.
2 Corinthians 2:14

Angels, from the realms of glory,
wing your flight o'er all the earth;
you who sang creation's story,
now proclaim Messiah's birth:
Come and worship, come and worship,
worship Christ, the newborn King.

Angels, from the Realms of Glory
James Montgomery

P romotion for Christmas sales seems to begin long
before summer is over. During a recent visit to a department store, I noticed several employees busily

setting up displays of the store's promotional Christmas bears. The bears wore cute plaid shirts and red overalls.

Several days later, when I looked at the completed displays, they reminded me of a story I heard years ago about a brown teddy bear that sat high on a department store shelf. The store was a well-known one that generally stocked up-to-date, first-quality merchandise.

This particular bear had a very pretty face and wore bib overalls and a plaid shirt, but the button that secured one strap was missing. The strap fell by his side, causing the bib to drop over his chest. It was obvious he had been there awhile.

The story had a happy ending when one day a little girl spotted him on the shelf and begged her mother to purchase him. The clerk pointed out that the price had been reduced since he was a little rumpled, and one button was missing. The child insisted that he was the one she wanted and finally persuaded her mother to buy him. She was overheard saying, as she cuddled the bear in her arms, "Oh, I love you. You'll feel better when you have a new button."

Christopher Morley once said that if people were given five minutes' warning before sudden death, "Every telephone would be busy with people trying to call other people to stammer that they loved them." Perhaps they would also be apologizing for the time they had neglected to care for them and would be asking for their forgiveness.

Love, kindness, courage, forgiveness, and mercy are not to be purchased in a Quick Mart or department store. They are developed through prayer and loving care for those who need compassion.

"Wing your flight o'er all the earth," may sound like a catch phrase to use for commissioning a satellite into orbit, but actually these words were penned by James Montgomery, a gifted poet and writer of more than 400 hymns. Through this hymn he calls each of us to share his missionary zeal and compassion for others by joining in with the angels in proclaiming Christ's birth.

Prayer: God, give us the vision and the knowledge to keep your Gospel alive, not only by proclaiming your birth but also by sharing your love with others. Remind us that expressions of love, even sewing on buttons, are the best gifts we can give each other during the Christmas season and throughout the year. Amen.

The Love Song Which They Bring

And suddenly there was with the angel
a multitude of the heavenly host praising God
and saying,
> *"Glory to God in the highest,*
> *and on earth peace . . ."*
Luke 2:13–14

Two thousand years of wrong;
And man, at war with man, hears not
The love song which they bring:
O hush the noise, ye men of strife,
And hear the angels sing!

It Came Upon the Midnight Clear
Edmund H. Sears

The first sound of Christmas heard by anyone was an angel's voice that broke the silent night of some shepherds out on the Judean hillside. When the shepherds suddenly awoke, they were filled with fear and needed the brief response, *"Be not afraid; for behold I bring*

you good news of great joy which will come to all the people."
(Luke 2:10)

Why did God choose angels to sing his love song? No one really knows, but history tells us that angels have always been a part of the religious scenery in most parts of the world. "The idea of angels generally arose amongst people who had magnificent and exalted visions of God," wrote Ross W. Marrs. "God seemed so holy that he himself could hardly afford to make a direct personal contact with mere people and the world." Whatever the reason, the angels came as heralds of the great event. They came singing a song of love that was to find response deep in our hearts.

The story is told about a young orphan girl who was lonely, unloved, and often misunderstood. Her behavior irritated the orphanage administrator, who finally resolved to find some excuse to have her transferred. One day, an attendant came running to the office to say that the girl had written a note and put it in the shrubbery near the street. Assuming this was an answer to the dilemma, the administrator ordered that the note be brought to her. To her dismay, the note read: "To whoever finds this, I love you!" In the book of Hebrews, we are advised to *"Let brotherly love continue. Do not neglect to show hospitality to strangers, for thereby some have entertained angels unawares."* (Hebrews 13:1–2)

The song the angels sang was a love song , and Christmas is their love story. It is a drama of divine-human love with a magnetic tug on all our hearts. It reminds us over and over again that the best and greatest gift anyone can give or receive is love.

The Love Song Which They Bring

Some of us may be fearful, disheartened, and perhaps disillusioned by the realities of today's world. But listen! There is a love song coming through our changing and noisy times. Into these gloomy days the song of angels—the love song of Bethlehem—again comes to remind us that God's will is for lives filled with love and a world of peace and good will.

> O *rest beside the weary road,*
> *And hear the angels sing!*

Prayer: O God, we thank you for angels who gave us these gifts of song. Open our hearts that they may be filled with the spirit of love and the joy and wonder of his coming. Amen.

Wondrous Star, Lend Thy Light

The light shines in the darkness, and the darkness has not overcome it.

John 1:5

Silent night, holy night,
wondrous star, lend thy light;
with the angels let us sing,
alleluia to our King;
Christ the Savior is born,
Christ the Savior is born.

Silent Night, Holy Night
Joseph Mohr

S ince time began, individuals have watched the stars at night. Sitting around campfires, they often told stories of pictures the stars seemed to make in the skies. They gave names to some of the groups of stars, names we still use today: Orion, the Milky Way, the Big Dipper. The Arabs used one of the smallest stars in the Big Dipper to test their eyesight.

Wondrous Star, Lend Thy Light

As people watched the stars night after night, and year after year, they learned how dependable they were, always appearing in a certain spot in the sky, at a certain time of the month, in a certain month of the year. Long before there were clocks or calendars, people used the stars to tell the seasons and the time. Travelers and sailors used the stars to guide them on their journey. The darker the night, the brighter the stars seemed to shine.

God used a star to guide the Wise Men in their search for the King.

> *When they* (the Wise Men) *had heard the king they went their way; and lo, the star which they had seen in the East went before them, till it came to rest over the place where the child was.*
> Matthew 2:9

It was a dark night indeed when Mary bore Jesus. It was a dark time for nations and empires and cultures. It was a dark time for individuals as well. Into that ever deepening darkness, a star shone over where the child lay, and the light of the world began to shine.

The glory of Christmas is not only that the light shines in the darkness as evidence that God loves us, but also that the darkness has never put it out; this is evidence that God is ever Lord of life and victor over the darkness.

Tonight, darkness will come as it does every night. But most of us will not be afraid or confused. We do not rely on the stars for light, but we have become accustomed to the cycle of daylight and darkness. Flashlights and candles will be used to provide light should the electricity fail, and streetlights and automobile lights will guide us when we travel. Although we may not depend on them for light, let us never forget that, just as the stars shine in the darkened skies, so the power and love of God will continue to guide those who seek him.

Yet in thy dark streets shineth
The everlasting light;
The hopes and fears of all the years
Are met in thee tonight.
Phillips Brooks

Prayer: Amid the world's darkness, O God, we seek the light of the Bethlehem star to guide us and provide hope for the days that lie ahead. Amen.

Let Every Heart Prepare Him Room

. . . I was a stranger and you welcomed me . . .
Matthew 25:35

Joy to the world, the Lord is come!
Let earth receive her King;
let every heart prepare him room,
and heaven and nature sing,
and heaven and nature sing,
And heaven, and heaven and nature sing.

Joy to the World
Isaac Watts

Christ comes to the most unusual kinds of people. The Christmas story tells us that the first visitors to greet him from the outside were shepherds and Wise Men. Here we have the humblest persons on one hand and the most learned on the other. Throughout his ministry he met people in unusual places: Matthew at the seat of customs, Peter at the fishing boat, a woman at the well,

Zacchaeus in a sycamore tree, and Mary and Martha in their home. He spent time with people involved in the everyday tasks of life, and so it is with those of us who follow almost two thousand years later.

Christ will come this Christmas, as he does every day, to those who do the menial tasks of life like the shepherds and to those who possess the highest intelligence and skills as represented by the Wise Men. No one of us, however, will be totally prepared to welcome him until we rise above the weariness incurred in preparation and the smallness that allows us to believe that he comes only to those like us, whether we tend the sheep or serve in the highest places of government.

Tolstoy told of the cobbler who looked for the coming of Christ into his shop. All day he watched. He saw a woman who needed food, so he shared his food with her. A boy entered who needed help, and he gave him assistance. Someone was cold, and the cobbler gave him the warmth of his stove. In the evening the cobbler wept because Christ had not come. It was then that he heard a voice that convinced him Christ had indeed visited his shop. He was there with the woman who needed food, the boy who needed compassion, and the shivering man who warmed himself by the stove.

Bethlehem was a busy, crowded town that night when Jesus was born. The people of Bethlehem were not necessarily hostile people. But they were busy! With great throngs pressing into town, requiring and often demanding attention, every place of lodging was filled. Apparently, Joseph and Mary had not made reservations, much less guaranteed them for six o'clock arrival. But an innkeeper did offer his stable, making it as comfortable as he could, considering the demands on his time and resources.

"At the inn they crowded Christ out because they never guessed who he would be," wrote Harry Emerson Fosdick in his *Riverside Sermons*. "But we have no such excuse. We know Jesus. Have we not come from homes where His spirit made a radiance in the faces of those we love?"

The question is, have we gained any clearer vision of how and when he comes? Will our hearts and homes be prepared to receive him, or will he need reservations?

Prayer: You have visited us on many occasions, O Lord, and found no resting place because our lives have been over-crowded with useless hurrying and preoccupation with the trivial. Try us again just now. We have prepared room for you. Amen.

Selected Sources

Chalice Hymnal. St. Louis: Chalice Press, 1995.

Fosdick, Harry Emerson. *Meditations from the Manhood of the Master.* New York: Association Press, 1966.

Hill. Caroline Miles. *The World's Great Religious Poetry.* New York: The Macmillan Company, 1923.

Hymnbook for Christian Worship. St. Louis: The Bethany Press, 1970.

Hymns for the Family of God. Nashville: Paragon Associates, Inc., 1976.

One Hundred Sacred Favorites. Compiled by Norman Johnson. Grand Rapids, Mich.: Singspiration Music, 1973.

Phillips, J.B. *Good News: Thoughts on God and Man.* New York: The Macmillan Company, 1963.

Prochnow, Herbert V., ed., *A Treasury of Inspiration: Illustrations, Quotations, Poems and Selections:* Grand Rapids, Mich.: Baker Book House, 1958.

The Way. An illustrated edition of *The Living Bible.* Wheaton, Ill: Tyndale House Publishers, 1971.

Worship and Service Hymnal for Church, School and Home. Carol Stream, Ill.: Hope Publishing Company, 1973.

Alphabetical Index of Hymns by Title

Alphabetical Index of Hymns by Title

Topical Index for Meditations